# The Meaning of the Mundane

By

R. W. Turner

Copyright © 2024 by R. W. Turner

ALL RIGHTS RESERVED

### Notice of Copyright

No part of this book may be reproduced, distributed, or transmitted in any form or by any means without the prior written permission of the Author, except in the case of brief quotations embodied in critical reviews and certain other noncommercial uses permitted by copyright law.

To request permission, contact rwturner2024@outlook.com.

Edited By:
**R. W. Turner**

Printed By:

Published By
**R. W. Turner**

ISBN Hardcover: 979-8-32740-955-2
ISBN Paperback: 979-8-89170-064-2

Published in the United States of America
First Edition, June 2024
10 9 8 7 6 5 4 3 2 1

# Table of Contents

Author's Note .................................................................... ix
To Whom I Love ............................................................... 1
A Great Moment ............................................................... 2
A Heartbeat ...................................................................... 3
I Stay for You .................................................................... 4
A Set Command ............................................................... 5
A Time Rift ....................................................................... 6
As Seconds Go By ............................................................ 7
Life .................................................................................... 8
Conquering the World ..................................................... 9
The Birth of the Death of Dawn ................................... 10
Life's Recollection .......................................................... 11
The Day Before the Day After ....................................... 13
The Ocean ...................................................................... 14
The Pledge ...................................................................... 15
The Pit ............................................................................ 16
The Secret of Time ........................................................ 18
The Traveler ................................................................... 19
This Place of Dreams .................................................... 20
True Dreams .................................................................. 21
I believe .......................................................................... 22
Today I Die ..................................................................... 23
From the Heart .............................................................. 24
This Place We Are At ..................................................... 25
A Poetic Templar ........................................................... 26
Twilight to Dawn ........................................................... 27
LIVIN .............................................................................. 28
The Past's Reflection ..................................................... 29
Death's Door .................................................................. 30
Where Time does not Exist .......................................... 31
The Key ........................................................................... 32
Today I Found It ............................................................ 33
This Lie that holds Me .................................................. 34
Words of Wisdom .......................................................... 35
The Fall of an Empire .................................................... 37
My Wish .......................................................................... 39
A Moment's Thought .................................................... 40
A Winter Moment .......................................................... 42

| | |
|---|---|
| By the Book | 43 |
| Why | 44 |
| Can't Rain All the Time | 45 |
| The Walkers | 46 |
| Confused | 47 |
| A Thought | 48 |
| Fear is Relentless | 49 |
| TIME!!! | 50 |
| Frost on a Snowy Day | 51 |
| He never asked why | 52 |
| If we can feel | 53 |
| Here Lies an Honorable Man | 54 |
| Imprisoned | 55 |
| Perfection Attained | 56 |
| Where We Stand | 57 |
| Little Man of Green | 59 |
| I Wonder | 60 |
| My Mind | 61 |
| My Hand | 62 |
| Things Opened | 63 |
| Stand | 64 |
| The Never-Ending View | 66 |
| Too Late | 67 |
| My Trust | 68 |
| Time Stands Here Forever | 69 |
| My World | 70 |
| There's something He knows | 71 |
| The Game | 72 |
| The Old Woman | 73 |
| The Stranger | 74 |
| The Knight | 75 |
| Too Far | 76 |
| The Meaning of the Mundane | 77 |
| Tomorrow's Illusion | 78 |
| Man's Greatest Flaw | 79 |
| And The Truth Will Set You Free | 80 |
| The Test | 81 |
| Conceptually Theorized | 82 |
| Detached & Disinterested | 83 |
| A Simple Child | 84 |

| | |
|---|---|
| Where Is It? | 85 |
| Vincit Qui Se Vincit | 87 |
| Does Life Have A Purpose? | 88 |
| A Work in Progress | 90 |
| The Predisposition of Love | 91 |
| What tha? | 92 |
| The Existence of Nothing | 94 |
| A Story of Life | 95 |
| Last Day of Spring | 96 |
| An Eternal Spring | 97 |
| Can Life Be Perfect? | 98 |
| Prelude to the Next | 99 |
| Can You See It? | 100 |
| Save Me | 101 |
| An Old Soul | 102 |
| LIFE | 104 |
| Time to Go? | 106 |
| Fun Times | 107 |
| The Man I Can Be | 108 |
| Youth Wasted | 109 |
| The Rabbit Hole | 110 |
| The Long Way Home | 112 |
| Genius | 114 |
| Enforcement | 115 |
| Irritable | 116 |
| Life in Color | 117 |
| Tomorrow | 119 |
| HURT | 120 |
| Immunity | 121 |
| I Live Today | 122 |
| The Greatest Question | 124 |
| I Hate Mondays | 126 |
| Onions | 128 |
| A Dreary Day | 129 |
| The Finality | 130 |
| The Dream of Tomorrow | 132 |
| Stone | 133 |
| Reality | 134 |
| Honey | 136 |
| God's Hands | 138 |

| | |
|---|---|
| Lucky | 139 |
| Mistakes | 140 |
| Change | 141 |
| A Beautiful Day | 143 |
| The World We Know | 144 |
| Forever | 146 |
| I Wrote a Book in a Day | 147 |
| Echoes of a Whisper | 148 |
| The Definition of Empathy | 150 |
| Don't Take Anything for Granted!! | 152 |
| A Broken Heart | 153 |
| Sleep | 154 |
| Should I? | 156 |
| Christmas Morning | 158 |
| A Concerning Life | 159 |
| Perception | 160 |
| The Remembered Dream | 161 |
| Can I? | 162 |
| The Unexplored | 163 |
| Winning | 164 |
| Dew Drops | 165 |
| Fall as a Day | 167 |
| The Minister | 168 |
| Changing the World | 169 |
| A Thought | 171 |
| Addiction | 173 |
| My Love | 175 |
| This World That I Know | 177 |
| Being Kind | 178 |
| The Perfect Pizza | 181 |
| Talent | 182 |
| Dinosaurs | 183 |
| At the End | 185 |
| A Gift | 187 |

# *Author's Note*

Dear Reader, I started this book at a young age. This poetry got me through study hall in high school. As I grew older, I decided to add something to my bucket list. This something I added was that I would publish a book in my life. With this being published, I can cross this one off my list.

This book is all over the place with the material. I'm not apologizing for that, it was intentional. My poems have been called dark and depressing; I need you to understand these are just words. There are a lot of poems about death. I plan to live forever, so these are just words. Life is just too much fun. Some of these words rhyme and some of them don't; some have meaning for me that you will never get. Don't worry about that; don't let it stress you out. You will think differently than me, and that is good.

I'm pretty sure none of these have been published; I don't remember ever submitting any of them. Some are good and some are not; this is 35 years of writing.

If you like it, I'm glad. If you don't, please put it down and never pick it up again. This was written for family and friends - for all the people in life I have ever met. If you do pick it up and like it, that is great. I do appreciate that.

I thought a lot about the poems, but most were just word play. I'm sure there are mistakes, and people will point them out. Know this: the grammar may not be perfect, but the book is. It is perfect to me. I did edit it, and I found I could not change a lot of the things it wanted to change. Sometimes things just seem right to a writer.

I hope you have fun reading and figuring out all of the ideas. I wrote this book trying to write in different styles; I wrote about different things or ideas, but it always seemed to come back to time. Most of the poems have some time concept in them. I'm sure you will want to hear nothing more of this once you are done.

With this item complete, I will never write another poem. After reading some of these, I'm sure many will say, this is a good thing. ☺

# To Whom I Love

To whom I love,
And to whoever loves me,
To my heart true you shall always be.

For as long as I live,
And as long as I breathe,
From my heart, you shall never leave.

But as I grow older,
I also grow bolder,
Bolder in the complexity of life's simple dream,
Bolder to the point of knowing life is not what it seems.

Whenever I leave your life will continue,
But know this, I will miss you,
And from your heart I hope not to fade,
As the years turn into decades.

So this I leave with thee,
A gift, a simple book of poetry.

# A Great Moment

The greatest moment there has ever been,
I do believe was the single second when time began.
Vast in the knowledge of being born,
Already fallen, broken, and being worn.

Those who pray and those who see,
Live a life, then cease to be.
How can the world see such a nonexistent past?
And question even to the last?

We arrive, and the truth begins,
But judgment is harsh, especially from a friend.
We see things different, you and me,
But the truth one day, I promise, will set you free.

Death is a door that we all must face.
Not a Heaven or Hell, just an empty space,
Everything fades to a bit of nothingness,
No sins, No mistakes, nothing you must confess.

The greatest moment I think I will ever see,
Will be the second before I cease to be.
Pure sleep will engulf the mind:
Then I shall leave you all behind.

Cold though it may be,
I would hate to believe and never see,
And if seen my mind will thaw,
Retract and confess what I saw.

Truth be known, I'll never sway,
I still feel it right to think this way.
Though I know all may laugh,
Maybe the greatest moment that will be,
Is the moment where I am truly me?

# A Heartbeat

A heartbeat away from death immortality
A second away from exiting reality
Enduring such a pain as the coming day
Has set me on my narrow way
Coping with the pain
As someone who is insane
Never remembering the past
In hopes of peace at last
And as the coming day approaches
My heart does fade
And then becomes a spade.

# **I Stay for You**

I could stand before my god.
I could spend my last breath.
I could go where time stands forever,
In a cascading waterfall of emotional bliss,
Where all eternity is but a dream.

A beautiful dream,
One of unbound sight, sense, and understanding,
One of unique and unimaginable pleasures.
Yes, I could go
And walk with the few,
"But I Stay for You."

# A Set Command

A time is given,
The command is set,
The hour is here,
The day I fear.

The simple lie,
Of a truth that is known,
Of one who is not deserving,
Of the majestic throne.

And all is good,
This is the way,
This is what has been given,
This is what we will say.

The second I stop,
Is the second I die,
Then I wait,
For someone to cry.

If no one cries,
Then my life was a waste,
And then a second later,
I will exit this place.

For a second which is eternity,
I wait for judgment,
After eternity is gone,
I will be alone,
Immortality is definite,
Realistically infinite.

# A Time Rift

The first second I was there,
The next second I was gone,
The day eternity made fun of infinity.

All the universe stopped and listened,
To time and its discrepancies,
Not knowing if it was the ending or the beginning.

As the second stopped between the first and the next,
Immortality seemed inevitable,
With no one wanting it to last.

The last second the universe ever heard,
Was the second sound of time,
And time considered the first second which was the inevitable.

The first second is now,
And eternity apologized to infinity,
The universe now begins,
And here I am,
What was once the inevitable, now reality,
A second time of immortality.

# As Seconds Go By

I find myself waiting for the exact second
Which would allow me a moment.
A moment of what is not known,
But what is a moment but a second,
And the second the moment is over,
I'll wait another second for the first,
For the first is infinity,
Infinity immortality,
With one exception,
You can't stay first forever,
Therefore no one is immortal,
And infinity cannot be reached.

# **Life**

Time compensated in equality,
Catapulted by the next event,
Synthesized too many ways,
Rolled and compacted in measurement,
Which never will we see.
Only theorized to an extent,
Eventually never to be.

The only moment of our existence we ever knew,
Was filled with confusion about what to do.
Always considering we would be.
But foolish enough to not foresee.
Only to live for the day,
No one strong enough to truly say.

Nonstop, continuous, and everlasting.
Nonstop destruction,
Continuous support of inadequacy,
And the everlasting destructive nature of the human existence.

Intelligent!
No!
Ignorant to all that time has shown us in our existence.
Truly only theorized.
Too blind to see,
Eventually never to be.

# Conquering the World

All the wisdom & all the worries,
All the facts & all the testimony,
I'll still the world or I'll let it be.

All the people & all their sorrow,
All the books & still I'm lonely,
I'll still the world or it will still me.

All the wind & all the snow flurries,
All the rain & it seems sunny,
I'll steal the world or I'll leave it be.

All the days & all my stories,
All the nights & none seem funny,
I'll steal the world or it will steal me.

All the places & all of my worries,
All the land & all want money,
I'll see the world or I'll let it be.

All the time & I can't stop the snow flurries,
All my efforts & all people seem phony,
I'll conquer the world, or it will kill me.

# The Birth of the Death of Dawn

To be present at the birth of the death of dawn,
So the day can see dusk,
And at dusk's ending light,
The year's end sees a century's worth of decades in a moment.
Infinity and immortality forever stand in the future,
Sensing tomorrow is the next day of the past
Never knowing which would be the last,
And as time reveals secrets from start to end,
Yesterday looks to tomorrow for the present to begin.
And I capture for a single second
The only millennium time will let me see,
Possibly the greatest moment there will ever be.

# Life's Recollection

I sometimes recall a state of foolishness.
I notice everything but the obvious.

To know what mysteries tomorrow will bring,
But not being able to alter the outcome of anything.

I stand at the brink of destruction.
Walking a fine line between two parallel walls.

Perched on one wall is a little boy, whose name cannot be defined.
A wall with an illumination that exceeds anything the imagination can comprehend,
The innocence of the world upon his shoulders,
Oblivious to human mental boulders,
This boy is omnipotent.
A look of pure joy and happiness
Understanding the importance of everything, knowing nothing of regress.

I ask for the meaning of everything I see.
To know the one truth the world has yet to define,
But to my dismay, he says, "You're not ready yet.
You still have many miles ahead; I'd have to bet."

I found myself backwards, facing another wall crumbling and falling apart.
Upon it sits an old man who looked far older than any I'd ever seen.
Decrepit beyond belief, this wall which will now haunt me forever.
The old man spoke with intelligence never heard by the human ear.
Surely, I thought, he could settle my fear.

I ask for the meaning of everything I see.
He says, in a voice not heard, but meant only for me,
"To know the one truth the world has yet to define,
To find what you seek, follow this line."

Finally, I found myself perched upon a wall meant only for me.
Covered with my memories and the future events to be,
I sat and wondered if this was where life would set me free.
I sat here upon this wall and I lost my sanity.

# The Day Before the Day After

The day before the day after
Was the only day I ever missed.
I've never seen anything so ordinary as time,
I've never thought of anything without it.
As time exists, then so do I.
Time seems constant,
As do all other things.
Can you destroy an atom?
In me holds all the power of the universe,
And every event that has ever occurred.
The day before the day after was never there,
Or was it really a day,
What was that fateful hour or second
Before the universe sprang into existence.
What force took part in the most powerful explosion of all?

Would an answer give clarification to the human mind?
Would the human mind be able to conceive thought along these lines?
Would these lines give purpose to an entity of self-righteous non-goal-driven fools?

I think the answer would be no.
I find myself wishing every day this were not so,
But the fact still remains,
The day before the day after still maintains.

# The Ocean

Dark on the most famous beach in the world,
And here I am, watching the waves roll.
When I look in any other direction, I see lights,
Brilliant golden lights,
And then, when I look into the ocean, I see darkness.
A complete darkness,
I see another universe,
A mysterious universe,
With the waves daring me to enter,
I can hear them taunting me now.

I could walk into the ocean,
And maybe I'd make it to the other side,
But I know the ocean has many perils,
And the waves have won.

As I live and breathe in this world that we conceive,
I know I could walk into the ocean,
And **MAYBE** I would make it to the other side.

# The Pledge

Every breath you take, I will take along with you,
And with every breath I take, I will pledge my love for you.

The water and wine you drink, I will give to you,
And this entire world I shall pledge for you.

In my eyes this vision of splendor will hold no altitude
For the things I will do for you.

Past, present, or future.
If you could have one, which would it be?
And if one could be seen,
Would it be the one with me?

Of everything I take from life,
The one thing I want most
Is that I take you for my wife.

# The Pit

I fell from glory into a pit of despair,
My lonely heart was broken beyond repair.

I thought I was on the brink of death
Holding to reality
By that which binds the human mind.

Who could have known?

Feelings of total failure
Not knowing details of activities unconstructed
Wishing the world would roll in reverse
Never understanding the worst.

I look forward to the future
But the future is now distorted
The world will end
Unfortunately because of something I cannot mend.

Who could have known?

The oblivious nature of a formal conviction
Is set forth by unnecessary restriction
Those who have seen this
Know this is something that cannot be missed.

I dreamed of a place void of illusionary distress
Lengthened to a meandering calmness
Never finding what drove her
Realizing too late this world is now over.

Who could have known?

I fell from glory
I turned to stone
I told my story
And then she was gone.

Who could have known?
Alas, I could have known?

# The Secret of Time

Time tells no tale of time,
Like the tales of time that I can tell.

I watch only to see,
A world where time can only be,
Time to stand still,
Time to share what you feel.

I watch only to be,
In a world where time can only see,
Time to feel,
Time to be still.

I let time flow through my hair,
And then time tells me,
I stop, I look, and I stare,
Of a time when all will see.

Time to go,
Or time to let go.

I let time flow through my mind,
And then time tells me,
I stop, I look, and I find,
What time should be.

Time is an illusionary figure,
Void of anything and everything,
Time is a tale that is invaluable,
In an indescribable nature,
I can only tell those who will listen,
And only when the mind has risen.

# The Traveler

I can hear the children playing,
But I can't see where they are.
I wish this is where I was staying,
But I still have to travel so far.

To the Moon and back again,
I'll leave tomorrow.
To the world I'll say goodbye,
Because no one else can follow.

I've been to the Moon and back again,
I've seen the sorrow.
To the world I'll say goodbye,
Because I leave again tomorrow.

To the Sun and back again,
This life now seems hollow.
To the world I'll say goodbye,
Because this I cannot swallow.

I've been to the Sun and back again,
But my life I had to borrow.
To the world I'll say goodbye,
Because I look forward to tomorrow.

I can hear the children playing,
And I can see where they are.
This is where I am staying,
Because I have traveled so far.

# This Place of Dreams

I dream of a place,
Which I cannot see,
And if seen, would cease to be.

A world of total health,
A world not immersed with wealth,
Where fear does not exist,
And temptation is something you cannot resist.

The day here is one of complexity,
Where every hour is a fraction of a second,
Every circle a square,
Everything that goes up does not come down,
And the shortest distance between two points is not a straight line.

Basking on a beach in the sun.
This place of dreams
Where I am god.
The alpha and omega
The only one.

This infinity I imagine to be
Is every second of every day, which I cannot see.
And what pleases me the most of a place that does not exist
Is the complexity of a world that will never be missed.

# True Dreams

I now have power,
I now have wealth,
My dreams have come true.

I now have strength,
I now have health,
My dreams have come true.

I have all I've wished for,
All that I want and even more,
But as the days go by,
And as time does fly,
All my dreams have come true,
But all would be lost if I didn't have you.

# I believe

Life will find a way,
I believe it can and will,
I find life funny.

# Today I Die

I die today,
And I'll be reborn tomorrow.
Maybe I'll know more,
Maybe the world will be better,
To think long ago when I was but a child
I had everything figured out.

So I die today,
And I will remember yesterday,
Yesterday I knew nothing,
But to think long ago at such a simple age
I was a genius.

I'll conquer the world tomorrow,
I'll be a god,
Everything will be good once again,
As it was long ago when I was but a child.

I'll swim the oceans,
Shark-infested with pirates and all,
I'll fly as high as the eagles dare'
I'll be alive in this world again,
Without a care.

I die now,
And then there is nothing.

# From the Heart

My love for you is from the heart,
Forever in love we shall never part,
Happiness it is when we are together,
I'm hoping and praying it will be forever,
Through the hard times I will be there,
To hold your hand and the love we share,
Always remember,
My words so tender,
My love for you is from the heart.

# This Place We Are At

Circumstances incorporated into ordinarily seen events,
Plagued by the innocence of society,
Ever knowing the grandeur of a rudimentary economy,
Prolonged and dazzled by the effects of liberalism,
Into the beginnings of communism,
Too strong and hidden to be seen,
But truly ordinarily, and maybe just a dream.

Fake or real,
Only a ploy or a single chance at a decision,
Based solely on preoccupation,
Alligated and agitated into precision,
Not understanding the near devastation.

Destruction and devastation,
Correlated into a systematic event,
Mislead by the total congregation,
Traded by what can only prevent,
Something so simple as a single citation.

Simple or misleading,
Simplicity changed in pure form,
From the hardest thought to mere nothingness,
Then to say this was the norm,
And not because of our foolishness,

Too saddened by the sight of our pure destruction,
Too maddened by the simplicity of our foolishness,
Too agitated by the misleading preoccupation of our decisions,
And to not knowing how to prevent the only true scheme,
Truly ordinarily and not just a dream.

# A Poetic Templar

Death comes to us all
Over a cliff
In a park
As the sun sets on a beautiful ocean.

I find myself flying
In a mountainous region
Over awe-inspiring breathtaking waterfalls
Flying ever so high
To glimpse the heaven that awaits.

Some believe life is a test
Some a dream
Those who believe in nothing cannot even gleam.

I escape to my world
A beautiful mythical island
Where I can taste and smell the ocean spray
This is my heaven, this is where I wish to stay.

As I sit on this beach and remember days long gone by
I remember the words of my track coach
As I round the turns of the track
Relaaaax, Relaaaax.

The memories of laughter, love, and joy
Fill me with a glorious light
And all the rest is forgotten
I know I will never see a dark night.

These thoughts will last forever in this light
And Although I know death is something I cannot fight
I know my world will always be good and always be right.

# Twilight to Dawn

Twilight to dawn,
Phases of the moon,
Dreams of tomorrow,
In hopes of being home soon.

Memories of tomorrow,
Thrown from the past,
Nightmares from the future,
Too unbelievable to last.

Honor and glory,
Too shaken to live,
Thoughts of a war,
That no one can forgive.

Woken to sights,
Horrified of sound,
Lasting to preserve,
The only peace I have found.

Unconscious of life,
Seeing the known,
Only believing in you,
Because of the love you have shown.

# **LIVIN**

The night has faded from its glory,
The dawn has risen in fury,
And the day has said its dues.

Now, here I am.
To behold the splendors of a world,
The world I know,
To which no one else can see,
And as I look upon it,
All is being revealed,
To those with special sight,
Who cannot be hindered,
By this world and the confusion in its light.

The day makes a try,
And truly, I know not why.
The words are lost,
Forever inclusive, not knowing the cost,
This I say to those who look upon
The night fading its glory into dawn.

Relentlessly resisting something so simplistic,
Timelessly contemplating the devastating.
Hold on to nothing, and this nothing that you hold, send it away
For LIVIN is truly the only way.

# The Past's Reflection

The past in reflection
Lies far and near.
All to repeat
Within the next year.

Not knowing reality
In hopes of today.
Wishing for something
Something to say.

Those who thought,
Thought they knew
What was once right
But went askew.

I hold my head high.
As high as the heavens above,
And I live my life
With nothing but love.

To those who thought,
To those who knew,
Pain will be wrought,
And the mind will judge you.

# Death's Door

Standing beside Death's Door,
Hearing a faint sound of what's in-store.
Resistance is stupidity,
You cannot fight what is due to come,
You cannot fight what is impossible to overcome.
Some delay it,
But the power fades,
As years become decades.
Is it arrogance?
Is it wrong?
To want no more,
And not be afraid to stand beside Death's Door.

## Where Time does not Exist

Then as the sun sets,
The day dawns,
And here I am,
Where every question is answered,
And the hour is eternity,
Never wondering off to the next,
Because the next is always now,
And the heart cannot beat,
The mind can only dream,
Dream of time.

And to all those whom I have passed,
May your dreams come true at last.

# The Key

It unlocks a door.
This is a door beyond all other doors,
And the mighty will overcome,
What the weak have done.
Those who have the key shall be the mighty,
And the weak will fall.
The birth of a new dawn will arise,
As the key opens everyone's eyes,
But beware, there is a restriction,
The simple classification of an addiction,
And all that has been and all that will be,
From then on, no one shall see.
The mind is the strongest,
From here the memory is held the longest,
But there is no presence of this memory,
As to all things there is a presence,
Mystifying as this may seem,
Maybe this is all but just a dream,
And to this all things will come undone,
When I pass the key through the sun.

# Today I Found It

Today I found it.
The gold in front of the rainbow,
By a stream with a steady flow,
Today I found it.

Today I found it.
The seven cities of gold,
From the legends of old,
Today I found it.

Today I found it.
The fountain of youth,
That repaired my broken tooth,
Today I found it.

Today I found it.
The Holy Grail,
Now I'm strong in faith, not weak and frail,
Today I found it.

Today I found it.
The four-leaf clover in the grass,
My only wish is that this day would last.

# This Lie that holds Me

Truth beware of the lie,
The only one that really must exist,
Truly I know I must die,
But the truth is I cannot resist.

Likely but not really,
The world knows nothing,
And the world truly does exist,
But the truth is I cannot be missed.

Living but not existing,
Still, truly I find myself resisting,
Contemplating the rest,
But the truth is I cannot be the best.

Forgetting but still remembering,
Something so unforgettable,
Too simple to be,
But the truth is I cannot see.

Loving but still hating,
This world that should exist,
The only lie that holds me,
Is, I will never be free.

# Words of Wisdom

Here I sit on the eve of the destruction of the world,
Quietly contemplating all of life's generosity,
Overlooking a sea of antiquated misconceptions,
Which represent every known aspect of life.

This is where I finally stop and focus on everything that surrounds me,
And by doing this, I find the answer.

Slow down....
Read very carefully.

Now look away very slowly,
Towards a place of new heights,
And in this place know that all things are possible,
All problems are solved,
And all questions are answered.

I also realized at a certain age,
Certain things should be instituted in every human being.

From birth we should learn to listen to all that surrounds us,
We should accept reality,
But at the same time we should be aware reality is what we make it.

Love the road you are on,
And live the life you love.
Think of everything at once,
And then attempt to realize all you think.
Read and learn the world, giving it a once-over,
And from this, learn to relax and enjoy the life you read.

At this point, I realize death is the end of a majestic journey,
And in this journey if you understand this that is written
You will be aware as I have throughout life, that
All is good in this world we love so dear,
As long as Rob is near.

# The Fall of an Empire

The fall of the empire gave nothing to what had been.
The nightmare of 100 years and fully with sin,
So really, no empire it would seem,
This had all been a terrible nightmare, a horrible dream.

Perception in the human mind,
Often brings consequences of an unruly kind,
And of these consequences we often find,
Our world that exists will eventually unwind.

We walk through life day by day,
Often not noticing the beauty along the way,
And at the day's end,
We let slip the beauty that had made their way in.

Show us not the line we must walk,
Lead us not for all will balk,
The human existence does not perceive the notion,
Of the vastness of this endless ocean.

The world we took for granted,
We thought we were in control of everything,
This life we easily throw away,
Was ours to achieve in every way.

And to know the power laid within,
We had the knowledge, the desire, and the conviction to win,
What we lacked was the correct leadership,
And the capacity from the people to be led.

The world tells many stories of great civilizations,
And from all we have learned destruction is inevitable.

If we could hold this power that lies within us,
And find a leader, whom the world could truly trust,
It would be the greatest moment in life that would ever be,
My only regret is, this is something we will never see.

# My Wish

I search,
Day after day
An invisible land
Which I wish someone could eventually understand.

I watch,
Day after day
Things unknown
Which I wish something would eventually belong.

I hear,
Day after day
Voices inaudible
Which I wish could eventually be plausible.

I feel,
Day after day
Thoughts unconsciously
Which I wish stood eventually to be mankind's true destiny.

I'm losing,
Day after day
The desire,
Which I wish meant my search would then expire,
But this search to which no one can comprehend,
For all things to which we can never amend,
Will forever proceed.
For the mind will never stop.
This day will never end,
And from this tormented eternity, here I will spend.

# A Moment's Thought

What foolish minds are we
To think for a moment we were meant to be.

To think for a moment.

A statement undeniably thought-provoking,
If only a moment were defined,
This statement is truly something of a find.

If a moment were a second, then I cannot guess,
But for the imagination it's something to confess.

Originally, I died before I was born,
The moment after the moment before.
Eternity could be the answer,
Or it could be the nonexistent period of time known as instantaneous.

I once knew exactly what we were,
From the first little atom to the complex structure you see before you.

I now believe no one can fully understand the complexity of the universe we live in.
The magnitude of the conceptual impracticalities goes far beyond mere man.
How thought-provoking could this statement truly be?

Let's think for a moment,
Can the mind be limitless?
What order are past, present, and future?
Is there a meaning?
What is the answer?
Is there an answer?

I have fathomed many things in life,
And in this life,
I think not only for a moment,
But for the moment after the moment before,
This is the only moment that truly matters,
And this is where my thinking shatters.

# A Winter Moment

Snow falling,
As if standing under a cascading waterfall of effervescent beauty,
The world around me engulfed in impracticality,
Eyes closed,
I turn slowly to imagine and imprint this winter moment,
Hoping and praying I can someday revisit what this has meant.

Evening's beginning,
Everything awash and basking in white,
The world still aglow with the day's ending light.
Mind frozen,
Realizing the magnanimity of this moment's extent,
Hoping and praying I will someday relive this event.

Wind blowing,
Lightly filling the earth with crystalline watery ice,
The world showing events that truly entice,
My being undaunted,
Knowing this moment will never be spent,
Hoping and praying from this Everest there will be no descent.

And with one last look at the beauty around me,
I understand the impractical feelings surrounding me,
I should say not impractical, but improbable,
I hope such a feeling cannot truly exist,
If so, this feeling will never be missed.

Moment ending,
The glow fading with the day's ending light,
The world's window slowly taking flight.
Unconsciously waking,
Slowly becoming aware of what was lent,
Wishing in this moment forever was spent.

# By the Book

And that's the way it is today,
But I asked, "Will it be that way tomorrow."
He said, "I don't know; let's just wait and see."
I said, "Living your life like this is a dangerous way to be."

He never knew what was next,
Never really even cared,
Till one day he was broke, old, and scared.
If you live your life day by day,
It's dangerous, and you will pay,
But if your life's a schedule and you live by a book,
You might as well give up, your life is already took.

# Why

Today has finally come.
Another year has passed,
And I'm almost through at last.

One more year to go.
Then life will start,
And from family and friends, I will part.

The day has finally come.
A year older and wiser,
A little taller and wider.

One more year to go.
Then I'll ask, Why?
Why was I in such a hurry?

# Can't Rain All the Time

Life is all about finding which door should be opened,
And once opened, finding the words which should be spoken.
Temptation is relevant only unto the week.
Retribution is something we all should seek.
Every particle is connected,
And in time, this everything will be dissected.
Control is a simple activity,
Unfortunately, few people can master it effectively.
In life, it depends on which door you choose,
And in time. we find whether we win or lose.
We all seek what we think we can never find,
Many forget our greatest enemy and our dearest friend is the mind.

With this being said,
The mind is at its best,
When the body is fully at rest.
That which cannot be conceived,
Is true only if you choose to believe,
And a belief that holds only pain,
Is silly, uneventful, and truly insane.
The life we live is truly precious, pristine, and prime,
What you have to remember is, Can't Rain All the Time.

# The Walkers

Do you remember the walkers?
The angels of heaven,
To us, the walkers.
Sad were we when came the day,
When the walkers left and went away,
But in my heart, I will hold this name dear,
In remembrance of that lovely, blessed year.

# **Confused**

I made a mistake,
Or maybe it's just fate.

I lost what I love,
The question is, what I lost it for?

Or did I?

I've got to find what I'm here for,
The dice are on the floor,
And it's not my roll,
If I lose this, I've lost my soul.

Or will I?

I know the love will never go away,
But never again shall I play.
More rolls than I can count will go by.
When it becomes my turn again, it may be too late,
But it's not over, only I control my fate.

Or do I?

# A Thought

The weights which bind me,
The chains that hold me,
This place I wish to be,
This place I'm sure I will never see.

I know not a thing,
And this nothing I know doesn't even give me a clue,
If life were but a dream,
In this dream, I would only think of you.

One thought,
A thought of you,
And as I die, the only thought in my mind
To me, would be the greatest thought in history.

# Fear is Relentless

It haunts me,
In my dreams and when I wake,
It's in all forms and not one have I been able to shake.
The dreams I dream are for those who dream of things they hold so dear,
And not one, dreams a dream and then has no fear.

It feeds on us.
It feeds on us all.
I can feel it all around me,
It knows just when to call.

A moment so divine,
All heaven and earth stands still,
To look at the one thing,
That fear cannot touch,
To be amazed,
To know at this moment,
A moment where everything is known,
A light so bright,
That not even fear can look upon.

# **TIME!!!**

If Clock's stop,
If people die,
Time will continue.

If the universe blew up,
Time will still exist.

Time is constant,
And will forever be constant,
WE ARE NOT!!!

If Clock's stop,
Time is forever.

## Frost on a Snowy Day

I see frost today,
This frost I see is with me,
It shall leave quickly.

# He never asked why

Six months ago Johnnie's friend died.
A drunk man ran right into him.
The drunk man got twenty years,
He'll probably be out in seven.
He never asked why.

Johnnie's son got kicked out of school for using drugs,
His mother talked to him constantly, telling him what to do.
The pressure of today was on Johnnie's son and he was through.
Seventeen years old and Johnnie's son ran away.
He never asked why.

One night, Johnnie came home early from work.
He found his wife with another man.
Twenty-three years of marriage down the drain
Johnnie was left outside in the pouring rain.
Lies and deception fooled the jury,
And sided with his wife's fury.
He never asked why.

Two weeks later, he was in a convenience store.
A man came in with a shotgun and yelled, "Hit the Floor."
The man said, "Somebody's got to die."
Then he picked up a baby who had started to cry.
Johnnie stood up to take a stand.
Then he held up his right hand,
"Take me instead."
He took Johnnie and put the gun to his head.
Bam! Then Johnnie was dead.

Johnnie was a good man.
Life was hard on Johnnie.
He never asked why,
Because he always knew.

# If we can feel

I stand before itemized instances.
Wondering the correct calculations of the chances,
Contemplating mass numerical possibilities,
Feeling for the first time closer to life's probabilities.

I stand before insurmountable obstacles.
Willingly losing interest in the world and its intricate vocals,
Calculating endless elongated equations,
Feeling for the first time further from my relations.

I stand before incremental paranoia.
With this I calculate my hysteria,
Constantly considering a universal betrayal
Feeling for the first time lost, weak, and frail.

I stand before illusionary detail.
Witlessly losing interest in helping the weak and frail,
Confusingly wondering through a mass of negating thoughts,
Feeling for the first time what the world has wrought.

I stand before the insanity of life,
Wallowing in visions of unendurable strife,
Can we find the way from here?
Feeling for the first time that the end may be near.

Wondering If We Can Feel?

# Here Lies an Honorable Man

A poor man,
Who had nothing to show for all the hardship he endured,
Forever at peace with the life he secured.
In Vietnam, he saved three men from death.
By doing this, he was shot in the legs.
In a wheelchair he would sit for the rest of his life.
I once asked him if he had it to do over again, would he?
He smiled, looked down at his legs, and said,
"I think you know the answer."
Two months, later he died.
And on his tombstone, these words were put:
I think you know the answer.

# Imprisoned

A bright star in the night sky,
An open window I wish to die.

A man in all his glory,
Stood tall, really a story.
I gave all,
But what I got back was small,
Now I believe in nothing,
And this nothing believes in me.
I turn a shade,
When I think of this life I have made,
But believe me not,
For I truly do not lie,
I live here today, and I try.

Imprisoned by what I do not know,
Never to see what could only be,
Return what is mine,
I can't stand, but surely I must flee.

Confused by what you say,
My life feels weak,
As I live without you day by day,
You're my love; you are what I seek.

I feel I cannot touch you,
You're a level above,
You have my heart,
I am trapped, Imprisoned by your love.

# Perfection Attained

How perfect and happy was I in life?
Let me count the ways.

Every child I adored and loved,
And if they asked, I would give the world.
I worked very hard in life,
And could not accomplish all I presented myself with.
I looked for the good in everyone and everything,
And wherever I was, I presented a positive atmosphere.
The love one person finds in another,
I found in the world around me.

I was told at a very young age in life that I would succeed
Because of my humility.
I have never seen this trait,
But I hope in truth that it is there.
I wish I could say I was perfectly content in life,
But I often found myself searching for something to want,
Many times, I found what I wanted most was the happiness of those around me.

Happiness in life is often attributed to the happiness of others.

I was always given gifts,
But for someone content, most stayed in boxes.
Yes, the gifts I received were unnecessary,
But the intention of those who gave them put them in a very special place in my heart,
I loved to read more than anything else on this earth,
With every word I read,
I get closer to the end,
And with this, the world I understood and could comprehend.

# Where We Stand

The world around me is engulfed in impracticality.
The human race is transfixed
By the media, politicians, and technological tricks.
With all the knowledge we possess,
We all still seem to regress.

Who will save this world?
Who will steer us on the correct course?
Would the world listen?
Would this savior be heard?
Can the human race conceive?

The world around me is mired with stupidity.
The human race is catatonic,
Purely ignorant and moronic,
And with all the knowledge we possess,
We still seem to regress.

Will we save this world?
Will the human race save their species?
What will transpire?
How long do we have?
Will the human race conceive?

The world around me is ignorant instinctually.
The human race is in time at a place,
And at this point we must choose which path we will face.
With all the knowledge we possess,
We still have the ability to progress.

The human race will not be the destructor of this world.
The human race will find their course and expand into outer space.
The world will be forced to listen.
Every day we delay is a day taken away.
Unfortunately, the human race cannot conceive.

# Little Man of Green

By the waters I have seen,
A little man of green,
Today he is not here,
He is gone like the Night,
If he comes again, he will be here tomorrow,
The wondering waiting is filling me with such sorrow.

Tomorrow is here.
Of him, I see no sight.
The waters have made a turn,
And are now the colors of a red fern.
The little man of green is gone,
And so is my heart's song.

# I Wonder

who you are tonight?
As I look to see the stars,
I can see you now.

# My Mind

Sometimes it hits me,
And then I think of how stupid we are.
When it happens, it doesn't last long,
But long enough for me to know.
I lose sight of things,
And for a moment, I'm blind
Sometimes remembering these things from within my mind.

It's only happened a few times,
And only when I'm in deep thought.
Whether it happens for a few seconds or a few minutes.
I see things simple.
I lose sight of the world and my surroundings,
And for a moment, I am blind
When I see these things from within my mind.

# My Hand

I know not what my hand may do.
I can only dream of the impact it may make.
My hand could feed a hungry child.
It could save someone's life.
It could write a book to inspire the world,
Or I could end the world with this hand.

Who's to say what my hand may do.
I could plant a tree with my hand.
The ordinary could be remarkable because of my hand.
We could unite the world with my hand.

To think we share so much with just a touch.
With a gentle caress or a light tassel of the hair.
I will never say as much as my hand shall.
I cannot fathom how many times my hand fell.
With billions of things yet left undone,
My hand can inspire everyone.

# Things Opened

I take a minute to open things that are closed,
The memories that are now locked,
But I can't remove the bolts.
To the words I want released.
What I want to say,
Cannot be expressed
Not even in a day.
Seems to me I'm depressed.

What I need to say,
No one wants to hear.
It can only be said one way.
It's the words they fear.
What I will say
Will devastate the world,
In less than a day.

# Stand

I stand alone,
On the rocks looking out toward the sea,
Listening intently to the waves rolling in,
All this time wondering where I am.

The day is gone.
The sun is now set.
Still alone,
The waves slowly getting me wet.

I look back and see the rest of the world,
Standing right off the jetty,
I find myself wondering why,
But I think I feel the reason is, they are not ready.

And the Night has taken me away,
The waters quickly turn from blue to black.
No matter what they say,
I can't seem to find my way back.

I now decide,
Who I am
Where I am going,
And when decided, across the waters, I shall walk.

I find I'm held here,
By what I do not know,
It may be the voices I fear,
They all seem to be saying Please, don't go.

I'm trapped.
Alone in the dark.
The day will never come.
The sun will never rise.

My life has run its course,
The world was my only resource,
Death comes to all,
To most as a surprise,
As it is now,
My heart dies.

# The Never-Ending View

Here I sit,
Alone in this desolate place,
My mind altered and often in a fit.
Strong I am, but to this I cannot face,
So here I sit.
My eyes seeing the never-ending view.

Few have told what I now tell,
Of a view never the same,
From this one-room cell,
Strong I am but I cannot run from the game,
So here I will lie.
My eyes seeing the never-ending view.

At times, I grow weak.
Living always in sorrow,
My life I shall seek,
Hoping for tomorrow,
And here I will weep.
My eyes seeing the never-ending view.

The times will grow,
The hours will chime,
To where they run, I do not know.
I only wish, faster they would climb,
And here I will laugh.
My eyes seeing the never-ending view.

Few want what I have reached.
Others stand away and nod.
Every day I hear them preach,
But who is really the closest to God?
So here I die.
Standing here in the midst of the few,
So close to this God and the never-ending view.

# Too Late

Through a person's life
They see times when they could only watch.
Always sensing there would be time,
But it was too late.

Taking a stare for a brief moment, hoping and praying,
But it was too late.

And for one brief moment
When the time comes and the sea rolls
You get a chance,
But you were too late.

Some people get one a life, sometimes two
And then again, sometimes it's too late.

For the one thing that's known,
And the times that have gone,
The senses that have shown,
The hoping, the praying, the brief moment of delaying,
And most of all, the second chances.
Is it too late?

# My Trust

Every day I see it.
It is my protector.
Through these pages all of history fit,
It is here, that I have my trust.

Every day its pages turn a hundred thousand times.
Its presence is over my house,
It's very close to my wind chimes,
It is here, that I have my trust.

Its words are flowing through the wind,
Wiping away all of our sins,
Freedom you will find,
It is here, that I have my trust.

It could be a sign,
Or it could just be there,
Whether or not, every day I see it,
And it is here that I have my trust.

## **Time Stands Here Forever**

I've climbed my mountain,
I've swam my sea,
Each day is finally the last.
Never to be seen again.
Time is now being collected and counted.
Friends are no more.
Never to be seen again.
The calculated is now processed,
And all is sadness.
Decisions being made,
Life's beginnings,
Childish endings,
Hearts broken,
Time stands at this moment forever,
Looking at what is the most confusing period of life,
Equal happiness and sadness.
Not knowing to be sad for the ending,
The ending of life as you know it,
Or to be happy for the beginning,
The beginning of life after the processed,
Time salutes, as I do,
All those who are the bravest,
SENIOR YEAR.

# My World

I take away the land,
And I give back paradise.
I take away the air,
And give you eternity.
I take away water,
And give you nothing but love.
I take away fire,
And then I give you everything.

I stopped everything for eternity,
And gave you the paradise you deserve and love.

I wrote a poem,
I wrote a song,
I wrote a play,
I stopped the world that faithful day.

To each of these elements to which I possess,
And your fragrance I love to caress.

I'll give you the world,
The world which I know,
This is my promise,
This is where we will go.

# There's something He knows

There's something he knows,
That no one else in the world knows,
I can see it in his eyes,
The way he looks at the world,
There's something he knows,
That I could never understand.

In years to come, he'll lose it,
He'll forget what it was,
There have been few that have kept it,
But there's something he knows,
And I'm praying he can accept it.

I can see the look in his eyes,
The faraway distant stare,
As of something great and humorous in thin air,
And then I know,
There's something he knows.

# The Game

The diamond was glittering.
The day was here.
The bat was shaking.
It was the first game of the year.

There was a man on first base.
I watched the pitcher studying his face.
He threw the ball like it was on fire.
STRIKE!!
The coach stood up and said, "Liar".

The pitcher looked me up and down and then smiled.
He reared back and threw me a curve.
STRIKE!!

The coach was pacing the floor.
This was the one I was waiting for.
I looked at the coach,
His face was tense,
The pitcher threw the ball,
And I hit it right over the fence.

# The Old Woman

Down by the ocean,
There lived a woman,
A wise old woman,
I would often visit her,
And occasionally ask for advice,
She was old and always very nice.
Every day, there were hundreds of seagulls by her house.
They seemed to love her.
One day I went to her house, and she wasn't there.
The seagulls were gone,
The ocean was alone,
And as the sun set,
I knew the ocean would never be the same,
As the days to the old woman's house I came.

# The Stranger

Life can play tricks on the mind,
Sometimes you fall in a bind.

In the days of my depression, I walked the streets.
My mind racing for ways to solve my problems.
I have no money,
I have no home,
My life's over,
I'm through,
No one gave me a chance, but you.

One of those evenings I was walking,
When I came upon a stranger who was talking,
But no one was around,
He said, "I see it's hardship you've found."
Surprise gripped me as I asked, "Who are You?"
"I'm just a guy who looked and knew."
Then out of his pocket, two dollars came.
He told me, "The world now is all glory and fame; to live now and live well means to sin and be willing to go to hell."
"Hard-working men are hard to find,
Especially one of your kind."
At this, the two dollars he gave me,
"Here, go find a bed, and think of these words I have said."
The words after that still echo in my mind,
"To be a man is to live and do the best you can."

# The Knight

He rode through the valley as if he had nothing to fear,
With the blood of the highest nobles,
With a steed of golden hair,
And a shield of great appeal.
But this knight who you shall never meet,
Had no wish to quarrel over something so elite.
He hath ventured long,
In fear of not to belong.
When at last he was entitled to presume,
Not only to belong but also foretell doom.
In his dying days he set out on a quest,
Not only to go north but south, east, and west.
When at last his time was up,
He came in on what was his last word,
But no one heard his last plea for help,
No one knew what this man felt.

# Too Far

Here I stand before you,
I look as you do,
But different we are in all ways except one.

I listen at all times,
But I have barely heard a word.
I've grown tired and now I will sleep,
Then once again, in my dreams I will weep.

For you and for me,
Different we are,
As you can see,
The words seem so far.

Lead me here or leave me here,
Do not look or you shall see?
No one in this world is free.

You've gone too far,
You've said too much,
Different you are,
So you, I cannot touch.

# The Meaning of the Mundane

Disregard everything I ever said about the mundane,
I find myself transfixed by the wonderings of a life's story,
The life we live, to some, a life of shame,
To others, nothing more than eternal glory.

I bide a second more of life,
To live free and unopposed,
Witnessing others dealing with strife,
Narrowing the edge so close to disposed.

The day is now gone,
The sky is now black,
Time skipped a beat,
And I can never go back.

Night falls on us all.
Forever in a dream, every human will fall,
And in this Night, we find everything lost,
Forever in this dream, but at a perilous cost.

We are delusional beyond terms that can be defined,
We are sad, pitiful elements of a unique design,
To stand inches away from an oasis of pain,
And wonder the riddle of the mundane.

# Tomorrow's Illusion

I gave my brother lunch money today.
A forgotten dream luring me back to the simplistic nature of giving.
This everything every day I do chains me to an island of terror,
The waves seeming to rip my world apart.
Amazing how a few dollars could help or please someone,
Which truly I could and would have spared much more,
Without question and without care,
Here I notice the realist nature of an effect,
And what effects I can have,
But the dream is sure to be lost in a pit of despair,
And it holds me tight with its one potent message,
Naturally, everything is but a dream.
Chains and terror are a part of this world.
Someone could truly help many,
But without notice, what effect can I have?
Once tomorrow's illusion,
A pitiful dream's intrusion.

# Man's Greatest Flaw

Man's greatest flaw is in his innate ability to misunderstand,
To learn is a process to which the human mind may never comprehend,
Within this process the feeble mind often rescinds,
And this is where the flaw always begins.

We find ourselves void of reasoning to a certain extent,
Some find themselves void of reasoning in any event,
To combat this flaw we must think with absolute chaotic control,
Leaving one's mind open to all things evasive and distortedly whole.

We see things often not there,
In this our misinterpretations are often not fair,
Once locked the feeble mind is often remiss to release,
Even when seen, the mind will still not cease.

The only way to remedy this flaw is to be open.
To all things good, bad, or indifferent, be open.
Let the mind know understanding is in the situation,
Life is perfectly within causation.

Listen to all things that are said,
Analyze and know everything could be misread,
Move the mind with precise calculation,
Then go again and clutter the mind with a chaotic alteration.

Then laugh inside as the flaw is perceived,
Laugh because the world can finally be conceived,
Realize every man, woman, and child has this flaw,
Then understand and watch reality thaw.

## And The Truth Will Set You Free

Who are we?
To think this world is sour,
I've always been told the world is what we make it.

Who are we?
To think reasoning is an epithetical approach in life,
Would you have me believe the life we live is tainted from birth?

Who are we?
To think time is a figment of the imagination.
How can you believe that we will stand here forever?

Who are we?
To think continuity is always layered with undefined abeyance.
Can you believe time is forever changing?

Who are we?
To think and conceive a million instances in a single second.
Should you believe one day we will be no more?

We are an evolutionary anomaly,
That transcends all barriers of emotional tranquility,
Living day to day by structure aligned through absurdity,
Unfortunately, destined to leave a mark of only a minuet obscurity.

# The Test

Do we test today?
I say maybe not today,
Today, it is then.

# Conceptually Theorized

We see things different in every way.
We define these areas every day.
How is it that life must last?
How different is this from the past?

We forget the days gone wrong.
We listen to life's long song.
How is it that life is cast?
How different is this from the past?

We live contrasting all aspects of reality.
We notice everything else is only a formality.
How is it that life is way too fast?
How different is this from the past?

We elude temptation only to find.
We fall forever in solitude within the mind.
How is it that life is luminous and vast?
How different is this from the past?

We psychoanalyze reality for a show.
We then Google to confirm what we didn't know.
How is it that life must be recast?
How is this different from the past?

I now explain:

It isn't,
Life is what it is.
Realize this, and you're on your way,
Mistakenly conceptualize and realize life's delay.

# Detached & Disinterested

I knew many years ago that life's abstract reasons were the world's greatest show,
This knowledge that I knew left me quickly, quietly, but with a great blow.
Now I'm lost, never to see,
And I feel this world will finally let go of me.

I see no end to the midnight light,
And I do hope your world is much too bright.
My time I spend without any fear,
Day by day, and still not even a tear.

And as I spun,
I saw death,
But only for a split second,
Decisions based on faded memories,
From years of inclusive isolation,
Saved me from the inevitable,
Something truly unimaginable.

They talk about things.
Intelligent, or so they think,
I know nothing but the importance,
Waiting for the proper guidance,
And to those with limited intelligence,
Who can only see so far,
I hope one day you catch your shining star.

# A Simple Child

A Simple Child so grand in their art,
With young eyes, knowing no worry,
With a mind so bright,
Entranced by the intellect,
So small and fragile,
Whose whole life is nothing more than today?
The world is so small,
And then visualizing the world in an unobstructed deliverance.
Knowing everything and nothing at the same time.
A lifetime of worry not seen at all,
Playing outside in the rainfall.
A miracle to see,
This Simple Child was once me.

# Where Is It?

The more I think of life, the more I seem to hate it.

I exist         -   Birth
I feel, I hurt -   Life
I think, I die -   Death

Why?

I'm born, I live, and I die,
That's it,
It's over,
There's nothing after that.
Its reality,
Thinking different is delusional.
It's all chance.
All a roll of the dice,
All that happens affects everything,
I was born,
And as such, I have affected everything.
An effect so minuscule it matters not,
In fact, our effect will never matter.
It will be a great effect on our world,
But what a small occurrence,
The greatest necessity is an observance.

To this we shall never see,
The human mind, at this point, cannot consider the gravity,
We cannot consider the future with responsive nature,
We are weak-minded fools,
Too ignorant to take advantage of our resources and our tools.

It is funny people are afraid of death.
They need comforting thoughts that everything will be okay.
It's been this way all through history.
People are afraid of the unknown.
It is an elementary thought to believe in a heaven or a hell.
The god that is known exists and lives in us all.
He lives in the mind,
But none of this matters,
You should be concerned with the future that we must find!

## Vincit Qui Se Vincit

I push myself,
I strive,
But at this point, I am lost.
I know I can reach it,
But I cannot bear the burden of this cost.

And here I am!
All focus is now shattered.
Controlling factors are no longer viable,
All things confused,
Time wasted, elongated, and then reused.

I think I can tell.
At this point, life seems so different.
A multitude of misconceptions within a brief moment of true inceptions,
I find myself worried about so many things,
Slowly slipping in the mire of a feeble existence,
Stopping only for a brief glimpse of what controls the resistance.

I cannot think things through anymore.
I move on instinct,
I now stand where I have never been.
I wait for the second to rescind.

I wait for those who stood the test of time.
A chance given to everyone, no matter the crime.
And then to look upon those lucky few,
Who finally realized, who finally knew.

# Does Life Have A Purpose?

I have no purpose in life but to accommodate the joy of living for others,
I will abide their thinking and agree with nonconformity,
I will abandon my thought and sustain this human logistical train of thought,
I will conceive nothing but the simplistic.

I think my mind has an altered sense of purpose for life.
I find myself wanting to bask on a beach with the world around me,
Celebrating the wonder of life and enjoying this moment forever.

Impossible,
I will concede.
Portions of the civilization feed on negativity,
Forever lingering on a dark sensitivity.

I live for the distinct moment when I can get a slice of my heaven,
This is the reason I live,
I know everything else is a joke,
Something a blind man once wrote.

I would hate to ruin life for others,
But this is fact,
We are born, we age, and we die,
And every one of us asks why.

Everything in between is unimportant,
This is the life we live,
The good times are an illusion in a lake full of memories,
All show without the impact of a tomorrow.

I can dream the greatest dreams till the day I die,
But I still die,
Maybe I'm wrong,
Maybe there is a purpose to life.

# A Work in Progress

The blinding sun which glares upon me
Holds me captive in its rays.
The time now is one of inconsistencies and disbeliefs
Which I haven't seen for far too many days.
I step forward only to find, I move backwards.
The air surrounds and pressures me.
I feel empty, and I cannot stand.
I look, but I can no longer see.
The life I live is no longer existent,
The world that I know grows ever more distant.
I wake to find,
A place where there is no delay,
Every truth is revealed,
And there is no day,
The grass is always green,
The sun will always shine,
In this world that today, I make mine.

# The Predisposition of Love

Anticipated or agitated to the point of no return,
But to this, I believe in nothing, so I turn.
Here I leave, but still I stay,
And inconceivably now, nothing can disobey.

For now I look
And in a split second, you took
The only other thing that can't be shook.

This I will keep,
And joy will always find,
The heart which will always beat,
In a perfect prepositioned time.

For no one will ever see,
A world which can never be.
To love something so true
Unbalanced by the radiating beauty of you.

# What tha?

I find myself risking the only thing left,
In an ultimate gamble for everything,
Interestingly, I think to perceive,
Intrigued by the certainty of my vanishing.

To be known as an entity,
Today may be the day that I expire,
Toddling with unprecarious steps,
Toddleristic emotional tendencies evident to transpire.

I want nothing more from this place,
And consider all things here over,
I've lived my life to my command,
Astute principle of living too sober.

I feel I must convince everyone else,
But truly, this cannot be.
All I want now is to be left alone,
Secluded, sitting by the sea.

Everything I have is nothing,
To them, their possessions are everything.
Is their life a lie?
Or are their lies, life?

When we leave this earth,
We take with us only the things we know.
Whenever we leave, something begins,
Because of this, the world will grow.

Gone are the ways of simplicity.
Gone are the times of nativity.
Great things shall be passed,
Global extinction must be massed.

Truly, I know not which,
And this truth I know
Shall be the only stitch.
For the rest of you,
YOU SHALL REAP WHAT YOU SOW!

# The Existence of Nothing

Today I did nothing,
Which truly cannot exist,
For if it existed,
Then it would be something.

If nothing is a non-existent entity,
Then indeed, I am but a joke,
For I am sure that I have seen this nothing,
And therefore, I did not exist.

I contemplate this,
For this contemplation is something I cannot resist.
Can there be nothing?
Can a nothing exist?

I have been to this place where the world was no longer there.
I have seen this instance of abandonment.
The question I seem to be asking is:
Is there something after this nothing?

The answer that comes to mind is, scientifically, No.
But maybe before the mind goes, you see infinity.
Possibly the grandest of an exit show,
What dreams shall we dream escaping life's true reality?

Maybe now you will have the paradise always dreamed.
Filling eternity with life moments forever streamed.
The second after a second of reality,
The second before, a second of death immortality.

# A Story of Life

I read a book once.
Such a depressing book,
The events so confusing,
The pages gave way to a moment of clear reality.
Then, pointing to a tiny instant of clarity,
Then, compassionately, giving way to the end.

The past serving the mind so unjustly,
Remembering thought in such dim detail,
Seeking answers to questions too long,
Forever knowing the ending is all wrong.

And I dream.
The child who saw bright lights in the sky,
The night when all life would die.

Now take this as it is,
For life is nothing more than a simple quiz,
Understand success is in context,
Life holds no illusions for true rejects.

At the end, I saw things easily.
I understood the concepts.
The sum of it was brilliant.
It had its ups and downs,
Its Highs and Lows,
**But it was great, nonetheless**.

# Last Day of Spring

The end approaches,
This spring has been amazing,
Wrapped ribbon and bow.

# An Eternal Spring

Intrusion into a life of joy,
This life seems predestined,
Already laying within sequential events.

What path will I see?
Will I destroy the world?
Will I laugh, or would I be relieved?

Everything that had ever been would cease to be,
And everything to be, No One would ever see.
The misery of all things would be no more.
This misery would be on some other distant shore.

A realization of death is at hand.
Bringing clarity to which I cannot stand,
Life's joyful day ends because of this.
Truly knowing in life, I was amiss.

Knowing these things, can I continue?
Knowing nothing, can I miss you?
Keeping my sanity, can I stand this to?

Know this!
No One can have all joy.

How will I die?
How will you die?
Must I die?
Will I die?
You will die.
Why haven't I died?
And,
Has this already been answered?

# Can Life Be Perfect?

I saw a place in my dreams.
I may have seen God,
What it looked like, I do not know.
But I do remember what was said.
It came from beyond the grave.
From someone who was dead.

I think I know hate,
And this is why:
It has to be my fate,
I will not cry.
So for this, I should die.

Leave all of this for me.
Stay no more, but go.
I believe in nothing I see.
I believe in nothing I know.

Night has befallen my castle.
I will last no more than a day,
Life has become nothing more than a hassle.
What more can I say?

The best we can do
The best we can say,
Is only enabling,
When life is perfect in every way.

# Prelude to the Next

The sky has fallen,
The land is now bare,
The winds are still blowing,
Saying life is not fair.

Day is now Night,
And the hour has passed.
I saw a sight,
And then knew the world would not last.

Forever is now,
And now there is nothing,
I know not how,
And this how I know, has to be something.

The truth is now false,
And my theory is done,
The world we've now lost,
Unfortunately to the sun.

Forward is backward,
And never is always,
Saying nothing is real,
Means everything must be nothing,

I believe perfection is insanity,
Religion a hopeless instability,
Stupidity being a worldwide infectivity,
With everything else in life but a fantasy.

The prelude to the next is now,
This now that we know, is the thing that we fear.
Daily people pray, and they vow.
Wondering where do we go from here?

# Can You See It?

Ironclad in an offer of such demand,
Who am I to say?

I believe today is great.
Tomorrow may be rundown because of laughter.
Who's to say which side I stay?

Now to those who know of people and their obsessions,
May the world finally be at peace as they make their confessions.
I cannot abide living in a shoe box.
Who's to say where my future may lay?

Light, illusion, and the pursuit of all things,
Here I see a day that may be,
But to all those who, in time, will pass,
Live life each day, as it may be your last.
Who's to say what direction life will sway?

I confirm time,
And again, I see the past,
Which will soon become the future,
The present is just an illusion,
With a slight pretense of confusion,
Who's to say what price we will pay?

I wonder if any will find,
I wonder if, in time, we will see,
I wonder who ponders the inevitable,
Knowing everything tangible.

# Save Me

The rain will not stop,
The day will never end,
This I will drop,
And thus, it shall begin.

All that has been said,
And all that has been done,
Is now dead,
And evil has won.

For now I haven't the power,
To seize my final hour.

My heart is now black,
My soul is now gone,
I'm totally off track,
And undeniably alone.

I want no more,
I've seen this day,
This I die for,
Please I do pray.

# An Old Soul

"Hello there young man,
Where have you been?"
Asked the bartender, an older gentleman in the twilight of his years.
"The night has brought me in with the ocean wind," said I.
At this, the man smiled and brought me a beer.
It's late, time's fleeting, and there's something you should hear.
And so he began.

"Once I knew all things,
Now I hope I know one thing.
I was great,
But now a mere man,
I loved thinking of science and dreaming of the future.
I was obsessed with changing the world.
I believed I was put here for some greatness.
I now know I have but just a few years left.
And I've known these things from the beginning.
I have lost so much,
And I try to find what I lost it for.
A name can change the world.
I thought every day of the next.
I wondered, could I change the world?
So easy to say, but so hard to do,
Look not toward the Pain of tomorrow.
Is Pain real?
Listen to what I say,
Live your life fully, each and every day."

I sat there, I smiled and I nodded
Contemplating and acknowledging the realizations told to me by the old man.
He looked at me and said something I will never forget.
"At birth we begin,
We learn, and then we sin.
Throughout life, we miss a lot.
Everything else we somehow still forgot,
Always be confident; never be cruel.
Never forget learning doesn't stop at the end of school,
So know this and know this now.
Do what nothing will allow,
Show wisdom,
Show charity,
And don't let your life end in such disparity."

# LIFE

I stand before you,
Contained by a curious design,
Delirious of all surrounding elements,
Unable to comprehend or yet align.

I stand before you,
On the rocks of a long-forgotten shore,
Puzzled but inescapably captivated,
By an acquisition of a duty before.

I stand before you,
On a small island within a paradise undefined,
Void of all semblance of adequate measure,
Too remote a place, too unbelievable a find.

I stand before you,
Transfixed by the beauty of the billions of stars in the night sky,
Seemingly endless beauty,
Void of the contemplations of a human lie.

I stand before you,
In-between that which is given and that which is taken,
Confused in regard to that which is required,
Standing rigid and trying not to be shaken.

I stand before you,
In the days passing hour,
Understanding for the first time,
Gaining mind's insight and a theistic power.

I stand before you,
Entering the dark Vale,
Wishing for peace, tranquility, and freedom,
Hoping to escape the delusion of an eternal hell.

I die before you; in this I am not one of the few.
Let me repeat this!
I die before you; in this, I am not one of the few.
Everything living will die,
And to this, I shall not ask why.
This Death will be a transformation.
Into something different in definition.

# Time to Go?

Timings on,
It doesn't make sense,
I don't know why,
But can't stop now.
Won't be late,
I can't stop fate.
Does it matter?
Right or wrong,
Who's to say?
Take your time,
Enjoy this rhyme.

Time to go,
Where, I do not know,
Can you see it?
Open your eyes,
Life is one big surprise.
Live, Die, or become one with the rain,
Now think, and let your mind go insane.
Is it a mask?
A permanent marker of undeniable disassurance,
Placating the disillusioned on the feeble existence of a second chance,
And as the years tick by,
Enjoy life, have fun, and try not to cry.
Because, like it or not, we will die.
And as you leave this world,
Know this,
Matter, destroyed, never.
You shall be here forever!

# Fun Times

Open water within a day,
Captured my mind in a joyful way.
We believe in an instance,
We find ourselves searching and hoping for the proper guidance.
Theoretically, it has already been delivered.
Realistically, we are not through the maneuvered.
I question even to the last,
Wondering always to the next and never to the past.

Open water within a day,
Has captured my mind in a playful way.
Beauty abounds on the open sea,
Giving way to a creation which only the mind can see,
And here we suffer the most.
Clarity given, then retracted, lost minutes from the coast.
This is an event that which some will never see.
This is a great journey forever to be.

Open water within a day,
Anticipated happiness in its own way.
Such a journey will forever be attained.
Such a journey in the mind will forever remain.
We have moments which in life we bask,
We have moments that forever, will last.
The waters will forever remain open,
The sea will live in happiness I'm hopin.

# The Man I Can Be

I shed a tear for you now,
Respected above all others,
Through you, I became who I am.
Through you, I became the man I am.
And perfection is something most say cannot be attained.
I hold this place for you.
The person I looked upon was perfect to me,
The person I hoped to become and will always strive to be.
Words cannot justly describe what you meant to me,
Nothing could come close to expressing what was lost.
I write this here to thank the man,
Who in his life gave guidance and proper direction.
Who took a young man and gave him the correct path in living.
Living a life of honesty and understanding,
Thinking of you always, Pappaw.

# Youth Wasted

Some say youth is wasted on the young,
How can this be?
Is it because they know not what they have?

I believe it is different.
I believe people who have aged should have lived that youth to the fullest.
I believe every one of us can see only so far.
However, if we opened our eyes, we would find a majestic being.

We should not say it is wasted,
We should not say it because of youth,
If I say this now,
Would this mean I'm old?

# The Rabbit Hole

How deep down the rabbit hole can we go?

The day will always be bright, and never a problem will arise.
Knowing this, we must understand and not believe in lies.
Why do lies exist?
We do not dwell on such,
For if we did, the Rabbit Hole would be too much.

The world is pleasant and always kind,
Being able to see this would truly baffle the mind.
Why is life not perfect?
We do not dwell on such,
For if we did, the Rabbit Hole would be too much.

Turns out time is not slipping away.
For tomorrow will always be today.
Why do we age?
We do not dwell on such,
For if we did, the Rabbit Hole would be too much.

Love is everywhere and can be easily maintained.
Unfortunately having this, is not easily obtained.
Why does vanity exist?
We do not dwell on such,
For if we did, the Rabbit Hole would be too much.

Friendship is forever and can never be broken.
As time heals all wounds, it also forgets the forever that was spoken.
Why do we forget?
We do not dwell on such,
For if we did, the Rabbit Hole would be too much.

Deeper and deeper down the Rabbit Hole, and no light to be seen,
Then suddenly, the mind is completely serene.
Why do we worry?
We do not dwell on such,
For if we did, the Rabbit Hole would be too much.

Turns out the mind is the strongest ally we possess.
The mind is powerful and can comprehend with complete success.
Everything in existence resides in the mind!

We dwell on such,
For if we do, the Rabbit Hole is something we will never touch.

# The Long Way Home

Can a home be found without sight or sound?
Of course it can.
We walk in a direction for as long as we can, and then go back.
We walk in a different direction for as long as we can, and then retract.
We walk in a different direction for as long as we can, and then backtrack.
Each time takes forever and a day,
Each day is a lifetime in its own way.

Can a home be found within life from the Long Island Sound?
Of course it can.
We swim in a direction for as long as we can, and then swim back.
We swim in a different direction for as long as we can, and then retract.
We swim in a different direction for as long as we can, and then backtrack.
Each time takes forever and a day,
Each day is a lifetime in its own way.

Can a home be found with no ground?
Of course it can.
We fly in a direction for as long as we can, and then fly back.
We fly in a different direction for as long as we can, and then retract.
We fly in a different direction for as long as we can, and then backtrack.
Each time takes forever and a day,
Each day is a lifetime in its own way.

Each of these paths have benefits as well as an obstacle,
Within each, finding home is very possible.
Most of us walk, swim, or fly through life without finding home.
Needlessly, in different directions, we roam.
Each direction seems to take forever and a day.
Each direction, a life, in its own way.
The way is so simple, so easy, and clear,.
Try not to think so much about this, and it will appear.

To understand fully, you must understand this:
Home is where the heart is.

# Genius

I often ask myself about relativity,
And think about simple creativity.
A Genius is said to be exceptionally gifted.
Could all of humanity be enlisted?

I ask this because I believe Genius is a term that is relative.
Every being is exceptionally gifted in a way that is creative.
That which, is not known, is a gift.
Could this simple gift be the reason all will enlist?

All the world can be explained and defined.
Over the thousands of years, it has been, and then somehow it gets redefined.
The Genius sometimes pales in comparison to the other evident Non-Genius.
Where even those that are thought the lowest can achieve greatness.

I saw a man who had not a clue.
But this man did what no other would do.
Love unconditionally, without desire or want.
And we think a Genius is exceptionally intelligent.

Does it take great mental acuity to love?
No, it takes much more.
It takes compassion and a knowledge some cannot see,
It takes kindness and understanding that is utterly free.
The world has its definitions,
And people have their perceptions.
But know this:
IT'S ALL RELATIVE.

# Enforcement

The craziest thing in life is enforcement.
To some, this seems like judgment.
To others, this is nothing more than an illusion.
To this, I say we live by intrusion.

This intrusion that we live,
Is by no means something that we can forgive,
For forgiveness is often unjustified,
And truly, can never be synthesized.

Enforcement means something very clear.
Turns out it's an unbelievable, unbearable, catastrophic fear.
For some, this is easy to hear.
But to others, this is totally unclear.

Should we delay it?
Should we stop fearing it?
Should we wish for the end,
And never be able to start again.

Where do we go from here?
Do we disregard the enforcement?
If we did, at the end, we would know all life is nothing to fear,
And hold what we see as judgment.

I write this to inform you,
Enforcement is not something you should fear.
I say this in the hope you can be one of the few.
To live life and say to enforcement, screw you!

# Irritable

Family can be irritable on any given day.
Often irritable, no matter what they say.
Rude could not describe it.
They are irritable and in a fit.

I teach others to be kind.
I teach others to improve the mind.
To me, this is the way.
So because of this, I stay away.

They say home is where the heart is.
This can be any place.

I wonder how many children live this way.
Unfortunately, unable to get away.
I find this sad.
I find no reason in life to be mad.

Why so irritable?
Why so mean?
I implore you to undo this nightmare they have seen.

Learn to love.
Learn to be kind.
Leave irritability behind.

I dream of a world where all are kind.
A world where everything is aligned.

My family is not bad.
They are the only family I have ever had.
But, as irritable as my family may be,
I still love them, you see.
For in my heart, they are always with me.

# Life in Color

Many see life in Black and White,
Always bringing out the worst, always looking for a fight.

What if we all saw life in Color?
In Color there is Beauty.
The bright red of a rose,
Or the Daffodils beautiful yellows.

We would stand in awe, if we saw in Color.

The fall leaves with various shades of red, yellow, orange, and brown,
We pass these splendors without a gasp, without a sound.
If we thought about the Beauty it would be breathtaking.
As said, many see Black and White, and this is truly heartbreaking.

The greatest blue I have ever seen is beach waters, crystal blue, right before the turn.
I have walked miles upon miles in these waters, and the Beauty still amazes me.
I do not comprehend how some can still see this crystal blue in black and white.
I do not understand why some can still destroy this from sight.

I dream of fields of strawberries and watermelon.
I dream of shades of huge oak trees, vibrantly green.
I dream of Color, and the world in perfection,
And then I wake.

Beauty is said to be in the eye of the beholder.
Look around; forget everything you think you shoulder.
Clear the mind and understand the sight.
Please release, and don't think of the Black and White.

How do we get there from here?
One Color at a time, understanding the simplicity of this rhyme.
How do we understand?
Can we comprehend?

We do not live in perfection.
Life is not all Roses, Strawberries, and Watermelon.
It is hard and often unbearable.
But is it really, if we see the Beauty then maybe anything can be attainable.

Remember this: Life can be as fantastic or dull as you make it.
Always rise to the occasion; failure does not exist, and make sure in life you never quit.
And think of this:
Clear your mind from the Black and White or whatever makes it duller,
And live your Life in Color.

# Tomorrow

If tomorrow never comes, remember today.
Remember all the kind, loving words everyone had to say.

If tomorrow never comes, live in the now.
By doing this, you will have all the happiness this life will allow.

If tomorrow never comes, live a life without regret.
By doing this, you will limit the hours you are upset.

If tomorrow never comes, do not worry.
Remember, life is fleeting; take things as they come and try not to be in such a hurry.

If tomorrow never comes, do not cry.
Remember, all things end, and all things must die.

If tomorrow never comes, remember to give.
By doing this, it will make it easier to live.

If tomorrow never comes, don't take things too serious.
By doing this, you may find you are less furious.

If tomorrow never comes, realize who you are.
By doing this, you will become a rock star.

If tomorrow never comes, know that everything will be okay.
Remember this, and everything else will be child's play.

If tomorrow never comes, remember, I love you.
Remember this, and do all the things we ever wanted to.

If tomorrow never comes, does it really even matter?
If tomorrow never comes, I will never know.

# HURT

I HURT someone today,
This is a funny saying in the fact that the word exists.
Can someone really be HURT,
Or is this all in the Mind?

How can man claim to be intelligent when this word HURT exists?
How can man not understand HURT is something the Mind can resist?
It is a state.
One, many try to complicate,
In this complication the truth becomes misconstrued.
And forms into a manipulation the Mind has imbued.

Can someone really be HURT?
Did I actually HURT someone today?
Does it really matter?
And what would the opposite of HURT be?

Know this: HURT is a four-letter word that truly cannot exist.
It is a feeling that the Mind forms on occasion in an ironic twist.
Don't let HURT in,
And then HURT will never win.

# Immunity

In time, the immunity will perish,
It will leave like the wind.
This immunity that we imagine will one day begin.

In time, the immunity will flourish.
It will roll like a wave.
This immunity that we imagine will once again save.

In time, the immunity will nourish.
It will be fine as the sand.
This immunity that we imagine will someday be grand.

In time, the immunity we will cherish.
It will be bold like the snow.
This immunity that we imagine will always flow.

We strive to immunize the world and, in the process, deal with death.
We mourn, we blame, and some even breathe their last breath.
In this life we live,
We should learn to give,
We should isolate, insulate, and navigate socially responsibility effectively.

# I Live Today

I live today in hopes of understanding tomorrow,
And when tomorrow comes, I'll wait another day to end the sorrow.

Which way do I go?
What lies do I not know?

I listen for the muffin man,
Sensing the demise of the gumdrop button,
While hearing "Be Good" from the Gingerbread Man,
Loving Donkey's many Butt-Ins.

I must not cry.
I must not die.
I live for today because this is the way.

Where are all the gods?
Are they close?
Can they feel the day?
What is it they are trying to say?

How many moons will I see?
How many moons will there be?
What end is near?
Why should we fear?

I do not, I will not, I have not,
I say this because I feel this way.
I say this because I live today.

Therein lies the rub.
How can man utilize not?
How can today actually end?
Maybe time can actually bend.

How many worlds are there?
How many oceans have been drained?
Why am I asking this?
Because maybe ignorance is bliss.

Can such be answered?
Should such be answered?
Would the answers lead to more questions?
Can I Today, Live?
YES

# The Greatest Question

I do believe the greatest questions are always the easiest.
I say this not to sound intellectually superior; it is just a statement.
One where the intellect is never spent.

Why do we die?
Who am I?
Where do we go from here?
Should we fear?
Is Pain real?
Do we really feel?
How can this exist?
Should this exist?
How can I resist?

Does everything living die?
Does God exist?
How many religions have there been?
Which religion is correct?
What is the meaning of life?
What is Love?
Is Love real?
Do we really feel?

The questions above are very easy.
Each has depth, and each has understanding.
With each, the answer is clear.
With each, the answer is simple.
All questions have an answer,
And in time, each answer will be revealed.

One question I ask myself daily is, "Where do I go from here?"
Should this be a question when the answer is so near?
Maybe it should be "How do I get there from here?"
It's actually easy: look forward and let all fear simply disappear.

Now, I reveal all answers.
Leaving everyone with knowledge well deserved.
Questions and answers are created in the mind,
And in the mind the answers you will always find.

Some will say this is not an answer to every question, but it is.
Some will say every question cannot be answered, but it can.
For all those who doubt and all those who believe,
Now for an answer, which is this:
The answers and the world are what you make of them, and ignorance is bliss.

# I Hate Mondays

Days created are not days at all.
These days created, I guarantee, will one day fall.
Do the deer know of these days?
Do the geese know of our ways?

WE created the days, weeks, months, and years.
For all other creatures, the time above disappears.
We live day by day, counting each as a milestone.
Not understanding, it is all so overblown.

We have seven days in a week,
And each of these days has a name of which we speak:
Some after planets and stars, others after Gods,
And then Monday after the Moon, which is at odds.

Maybe at odds is not correct,
But Monday is the lowest of the group, as I check.
Somehow, Monday took the first.
With this, Monday, by many, is labeled as the worst.

The only reason for the label is the start of the work week.
What if work was loved; would Monday be a day you would seek?
What if there was no start?
What if, from the work, we could never part?

Each name was given by man.
With this, the name has a lifespan.
Day by day, they toil away.
They sense the fleeting of time, trying to keep it at bay.

How many more Mondays will there be?
How many more Mondays will we see?
How many can see through the transparency?
When will time reclaim man's heresy?
For all those who live in a time that is a haze,
I must tell you, I do Love Mondays.

# Onions

There are a few things that are great for you in life:
Onions are one of them.

You ask why?

Onions are packed with Nutrients.
They are loaded with Antioxidants.
They contain Cancer-fighting Compounds.
They have Antibacterial Properties.
They may benefit Heart Health, help control Blood Sugar, and boost Bone Density.

All of these are reasons I love onions, but the main reason is they are delicious.
And with this, I say eat away.
Let all the bad things vanish when an onion saves the day.
Onions are magical.
They lend to the mythical.
Maybe it should be an onion a day that will keep the doctor away.
There have proven benefits.
Most just look over the relevance.
For those who do not, eat away,
And know to your life, you may be adding a day.

# A Dreary Day

What makes a dreary day?

Is it the weather?

Could it be circumstances?

What about health?
Could health be the issue?

I ask to understand,
I ask to comprehend,
For each day is what we make it,
Because of this, we cannot fake it.

I bask in the Dreary Day's diminished light.
I comprehend and leave the fight.
This unsimple truth is but a myth.
Unfortunately, a tragic misconception that we all must live with.

But alas, the Dreary Day will turn,
Erasing the knowledge of the day as we learn.
For each and every second is knowledge,
And only knowledge can release the Dreary Day's bondage.

Have no worries,
This Dreary Day is easy to appease.
Just don't stress,
Always be positive and never distress,
Do this, and your life will always be a success.

# The Finality

Yesterday I did addition to simplify the answer.
Fortunately, the proof did not disappoint.
In fact, it was an acute abstract of the proponent.

Today, I subtract.
Tomorrow, I divide.
On a hilly path somewhere between where I will forever reside.

Tomorrow, I multiply, and then I add a constant.
I calculate all the possibilities of time and its involvement.
As I walk the path, I notice areas that have blooming flowers and areas that are void.
The hilly path is long and arduous, with many twists and turns with areas I wish I could avoid.

In the future, I will average the percentage of the additional data for logic.
I will analyze the theorem to abstract the fundamentals of the proponent.
As I walk the path, I finally understand it is all just psychologic.
I finally understand the hilly path is not my opponent.

At the end of this path, I meet the entity that I have been trying to evade my whole life.
An entity I try to give the data to,
But the entity doesn't care about the calculations, the possibilities, the theorems I have devised.

No words are spoken,
No sign is given,
The bonds are now broken,
And the discontinuity of the fixed segment, which relates to the norm of the vector, has been written.

I question if Death has a mind of its own.
I question if Death really does belong,
As I stand on this hilly path wondering if the finality of life is actually wrong.

# The Dream of Tomorrow

I live today understanding tomorrow may be a dream.
A dream that may never be.
This is life for everyone.
This is the reality we must see.

We talk to each other and plan on a daily basis.
These plans are never anything more than a dream.
A dream which we believe to be correct,
But not everything is what it may seem.

As I wake, the morning's alarm blaring, I understand another day is here.
This day was nothing more than a dream the night before.
Today it is reality, and with reality, a dose of appreciation does appear.
And once seen, we start the process all over again.

# Stone

Stone is very hard,
Although it can be broken,
This I have spoken.

# Reality

We take things for granted.
We think we are above others and we are special, but we are not.
We destroy, we kill, and we cry after we do these things.
We think that we matter, but we don't.
We are immature beings who believe we were created by something or someone, but we weren't.
We pollute and think nothing of the little sea crab that has to deal with the trash at the bottom of the ocean.
We are not as intelligent as we think we are.
We destroy our bodies through the years and wonder why we are unhealthy.
We believe the earth is ours, but it isn't.
We have not been here long; there were animals here much longer than we have existed.
We see only what we want to see.
We overlook the obvious and often get angry about it.
We are wasting resources on a scale never before seen, and we don't believe this.
We are not alone in the universe, probably not even the galaxy.
We want to belong, and often do idiotic things to get there.
We think people are always judging us, but they aren't; no one is perfect, most of us are constantly judging ourselves.
We are needy, and we constantly ignore those actually in need.
We call people Names, disturb people's lives, and obsess over information that could be false.
We speak when we should listen.
We speak when we have no idea why we are speaking.
We are mortal, and we will die.
Every word written here is correct; there will be those who deny this, but they are.
As you read this, you will think we can do better, but we can't.
Saying this may make you think there is no hope for the human species; at the rate we're going, there isn't.
Everyone should believe in a brighter future, no matter how bleak life may be.

Live a life of happiness.
Strive to understand everything.
Don't pollute or destroy.
Build things that make the world a better place.
Help as much as you can,
And please be nice and assist your fellow man.

# Honey

There are few things in nature as miraculous as honey,
This wonderful fruit - yes, I said fruit - is one of the greatest things in the world.
From the beginning, we must understand what compromises this delicious item.
To do this, we will discuss the bee.

This little flyer is active.
To say active would be a major understatement.
We must go even further with the word hyperactive.
Next, we will discuss the bee's placement.

They fly around and pollinate.
This is how flowers replicate.
With miles to go before they sleep and dangers at every turn being steep,
They do it again and again in repeat.

But this is about honey, not the world-destroying fact bees are becoming increasingly scarcer.
This is about an end,
Not the end.

Throughout history there has been pollination in one form or another.
There will be again.
I'm sure of this.

People worry,
They probably should.
For without honey, our world may be no more.
Don't worry too much though,
For in this world, there is much, much more in store.

The bee may be on the way out,
But I promise you something new will sprout.
Man may not see it,
But the world will continue pollinating; something will recommit.

# God's Hands

What god laid his hand on this earth?
What God did give the day birth?
I ask because I need to know.
I ask because I need to grow.

Can I grow without an answer?
Can I see without an enhancer?
Maybe I can,
But it may take a lifespan.

There is no doubt religion is right.
There is no doubt in the evil it will fight.
What doubt should man have if this is the case?
What doubt would man have in this place?

Can I die without an answer?
Can I understand this without an enhancer?
I think I can,
But it may take my lifespan.

How many days will this last?
How many thoughts will be cast?
Is there a right answer?
Can I find it without this enhancer?

Turns out, faith is the enhancer.
Faith is religion's advancer.
So believe and have faith in whatever you must.
By doing this, in God's hands you will be thrust.

# Lucky

I once had a dog; he was sweet, kind, and very playful.
This dog that I once owned, I loved.
He was a good dog and gave me much joy in life.
Never mean, hateful, or giving off strife.

I'm not really a person that likes animals.
Although they seem to like me.
This dog was different,
His playful spirit was always considerate.

He knew everything about me.
We talked nonstop about everything.
This dog was my best friend,
Even to the end.

As days go by,
We all get a little closer.
For a dog this comes sooner than later,
And as the day came, I dreamed of him standing by the creator.

As I woke, I cried.
I cried, deep and sorrowful.
I once had a dog named lucky,
That now I realize, I loved from a puppy.

# Mistakes

I have made many mistakes.
I don't dwell on them,
Most of the time, I don't even claim them.
All of us make mistakes.
Do not dwell on them.

Try to be better in life.
Try to do good in life.
Try hard,
Try really hard.

If you do, then no matter what mistakes you have made,
Mean nothing; each and every one will eventually fade.

# Change

Change can happen in an instant.
Change can happen gradually.
Change can be constant.
And Change is always Happening.

It can be exciting.
It can be scary.
It can be expensive.
And it can be hard.

The one thing Change can give us is opportunity.
Opportunity to do something great, to dream, and live an eventful life.
On the other side of Change is complete and utter chaos.
A moment that alters life in the most unimaginable way.

This is life, and this is Change.
We control some change, but of course, not all.
The world is a major player with Change.
The other is individuals and other life forms.

Change can be moving to the highest peaks or to a tropical paradise.
It can be finding out you're going to be a mother or a father.
As simple as running instead of walking.
Change is ever-changing, from one moment to the next.

The only thing that doesn't Change is time.
Time is constant and cannot be altered.
If this were possible, it would unravel reality.
Time is outside everything - all items, formulas, or hypotheses that exist.

Some fear Change, others love Change.
Then there are those who ignore Change, or they try to.
To this, the mind will only comprehend what we allow.
And this is where the next sentence is applicable.

Change is inevitable; it's what we do with this Change that is not.

# A Beautiful Day

A beautiful day,
I wonder what the next one will say.
We strive for all that can be had.
We live in an attempt not to be sad.

An ordinary day,
I wonder if the sun will stay.
We wake and still dream of the next.
We live and still find our lives perplexed.

A dreary day,
I wonder if the turning world I can delay.
We plan but forget the important,
We live and regret items that do not warrant.

A nightmare day,
I wonder if the world I can slay.
We forget what life is, however it may seem.
We live and forget that life is but a dream.

As all that has been said and all that has been read
Live life better and never be concerned about the day's weather.
Enjoy, be content, and love every day spent.
For all the wisdom that I have given, I love what this day has meant.

# The World We Know

People are weird.
I say this because they are.
Emotions are for the weak.
I say this because they are.

Some may anger at the above statement.
This is fine.
Anger away at what you believe to be crazy,
What you believe to be absolute insanity.
But believe me when I say, the human race will not last.

This time we live is but a minute moment in history.
One in which to understand would take a lifetime.
This has been basic science since the beginning of everything.
Strong cells survive, and weak cells die.

Why be angry at this fact?
Why not open the mind to new concepts and ideas?
Why not see things for what they are?
Which, for everyone, means something different?

This is smart.
This is correct.

People are ignorant.
I say this because it is true.
Humans are destructive.
I say this because it is true.

Can we change?
I doubt it.
Is this strange?
No, it isn't.

The way we survive is to stop wanting and just be.
Be perfect with a goal, and open your eyes to see.
For what is seen, may be understood.
With this, our world may be able to swim from all the falsehood.

# Forever

My heart fluttered the day I met you.
It truly stopped the day you said yes.
I find myself thinking it can be forever.

I find myself wondering your thoughts on the matter.
I feel it is commiserate, but I do not know.
Although, I find myself wanting it to be forever.

I ask, can it be forever?
How upset will you eventually be with me?
I find myself thinking it can be forever.

I'm really curious about your thoughts.
Can we be perfect together?
I find myself hoping and praying it can be forever.

All of a sudden, I am not sure.
We are truly perfect together,
But how long is forever?

The truth is that the heart knows nothing.
Everything is actually in the mind,
And love is something that will never be bluffing.
For this forever in love, we will soon bind.

# I Wrote a Book in a Day

Fortunately, I wrote a book in a day.
A thick book about thoughts I had laying around,
I lived an amazing life, but truly, who's to say?

I loved all things, or I found a way.
I loved every mystery I eventually found.
Fortunately, I wrote a book in a day.

I wrote of how to keep death at bay.
The science is there, the science is sound.
I lived an amazing life, but truly, who's to say?

I was born during the month of May.
I lived a life that was so profound.
Fortunately, I wrote a book in a day.

Interesting enough, I had two sentences by mid-day.
Then the words would not be bound.
I lived an amazing life, but truly, who's to say?

To some, the concept of a day will always fray.
Then, to others, it will logically astound.
Fortunately, I wrote a book in a day.
I lived an amazing life, but truly, who's to say?

I say!!

# Echoes of a Whisper

I hear echoes of a whisper in the air,
Falling meekly in a pit of despair.
Feeble beginnings mark the day,
In this place, where I must stay.
What price must I pay?
What illusions will life portray?
In this Indistinct and unfathomable reality,
A beautiful delightful tragedy.

I hear echoes of a whisper in the air,
Seems the world has not a care.
Feeble Beginnings are far and away,
I care not for this day,
I often wonder what thoughts lay,
But really who is to say,
I am well informed on the illusions life will portray.
Distinct And fathomable reality,
Sheds a realistic light on this tragedy.

I hear echoes of a whisper in the air,
And I cannot help but stare.
Feeble beginnings are come what may,
I find it very hard to get away,
In a world made of clay,
In a land that I no longer want to play.
In a dream of this reality,
A close-up, of this tragedy.

I hear echoes of a whisper in the air,
And I have not a care.
Feeble beginnings are a hard way,
I find I want to delay.
For if it was right and if I could sway,
I would; I promise I would, each and every day.
I now own this reality.
It Is completely my own tragedy.

# The Definition of Empathy

I give the definition of Empathy,
So sweet a verse that is of pure clarity.
"Empathy is the ability to understand and share the feelings of another",
To some, this is nothing more than a cover.

To others, this is natural and always easily done.
To a few, this is misguided until clarity is won.
I now give an example:
A child buys food for another human and is taught this is ample.

The child saw the man's plight,
And felt that feeding him was right.
Is the world empathetic?
Can it be sympathetic?

I hope so,
I do hope so.
With all of the world in such a state,
This kid showed Empathy with such weight.

Why was this done?
The kid understood his plight,
And immediately knew what was right.

Could this have been done any better?
No, I doubt it!
The kid used Empathy to understand what the man needed and got it for him.
This was perfect.

With this child being so empathetic I wonder what the world can be.
I'm sure in the future we will see.
The world turns as time marches on,
In a world where Empathy is in full view, not lost and not gone.

# Don't Take Anything for Granted!!

Consider the Atom,
They toil not but spin like crazy,
Until everything is hazy,
The electrons are even worse,
They have an intense desire to disperse.
No one should ridicule this propensity,
Because it reduces their density.
As for the Alpha and Beta particles
And such articles.
Too small to seem to matter at all,
Watch it – the decline and fall
Was due to ignoring the small but busy.
The emperors went around saying, who is he?
And the first counsel would say to ignore 'em,
They don't even amount to a quorum.
In fact, we don't want 'em.
Then along came the quantum,
To say nothing of the Goth,
And we all know about the candle and the Moth.
Only this time, the Moth blew out the candle,
But he was unable to handle
Things any better than the emperor could,
So knock on wood.

# A Broken Heart

My heart is now broken,
My world is now sad.
I wish you had spoken
Before I had.

I fear it is now over,
And I find myself hoping for a do-over.
My heart is now sore,
And it has definitely hit the floor.

My heart will always be broken,
My world will always be sad.
I really wish you had spoken
Before I had.

I know it is now over,
And I no longer hope for a do-over.
Time heals everything,
Unfortunately, we are time's plaything.

My heart was broken,
My world was sad.
I still wish you had spoken
Before I had.

Time progresses and we all move on,
As with everything, love exists, and then it is gone.
To each his own,
This is for each heart that has grown.

My heart is not broken,
My world is not sad.
But I still wish you had spoken
Before I had.

# Sleep

I lie awake as sleep eludes me,
Contemplating moments of the unending day,
Planning activities to live life in an easy way.

I think,
Therefore, I am.
Do you believe everything is good?
If not, do you wish you could?

The world is what we make it,
So make it grand.
My existence is minute
In the grand scheme of things, of this, you cannot refute.

As tiny and inconsequential as we all are,
It's astounding where we think we sit.
This place, we think we are, is not here.
It is a place everyone should probably fear.

We do not control the universe.
We do not control this planet.
We control very little in life.
Which is why, with little control, contains strife.

I think,
Therefore, I am.
I know everything is good.
I do not dwell on the above, as I probably should.

We live day by day and try to stay out of each other's way.
We understand in this place we cannot stay.
We love and hate and sometimes debate.
We actually live in control of our fate.

What is this fate that I speak of?
It is everything that happens in life.
It is every moment in time that has existed.
It is everything above that was listed.

I think,
Therefore, I am.
And suddenly, I wake.

# Should I?

I question myself.
Do I dare to dream,
And live my life to the extreme?

Daily, I laugh,
As the populace runs the course of Life,
Most broken, beaten, worn, and consumed with strife.

We are the Fallen.
To imagine the indescribable number of words that have fallen on deaf ears,
And to see the numbing implications that will fall for many years.

I still look forward.
What we do hear are things that are capable,
We cannot dwell on changing things that are unchangeable.

And still, I question myself.
Do I dare to dream,
And live my life to the extreme?

Daily, I laugh,
Because I believe we are born to true perfection,
Then this life we live consumes and fills us with greed, lust, envy, malice, and infection.

We are the Fallen.
There are those who can see with uninfected eyes.
Understand all implications and detect all existing Lies.

As I look forward
I dream of a perfect place.
I see the world working together as one human race.

I no longer question myself.
I dare to dream,
And yes, live my life to the extreme.

# Christmas Morning

Christmas is special.
It is a time of giving, of joy, and reunion.

The best thing about Christmas to me is the morning.
The kids get up and are all excited.
It hugs my heart to see them so delighted.

As presents are unwrapped,
The world's issues and problems are suddenly snapped.
During this Christmas morning,
Love abounds and is warming.

Excitement and Joy are everywhere.
Day breaks, and so starts the funfair.
As the morning wanes, the festivities implore,
And happiness asks for just one more.
Christmas morning always has one more gift to give.
One more happy moment to live.

Christmas is special.
Here, it always has been and always will be.

# A Concerning Life

I have taken many roads in life.
Some have been rocky, and others have not.

I have seen many things in life.
Some have been good, and others have not.

I have to think this relates to everyone.
Some have seen more than others, and some have not.

I have written a good bit of poetry in life.
Some have been amazing, and others have not.

I have fished the ocean and sailed the seas in life.
Some have done this, and some have not.

I have had thoughts about the entire existence of the universe that are so profound.
Some have had these thoughts, and some have not.

I have said nice things to people in life.
Some have done this more than me, and some have not.

I have said terrible things to people in life.
Some have done this more than me, and some have not.

I have helped others tremendously in life.
Some have done this, and some have not.

All of the above are life's twists and turns.
All of the above is nothing more than life's concerns.

# Perception

I ate an apple today,
It was a good apple.
I'm sure it was healthy,
But really, who is to say.

I'm thinking that would be a doctor.
Do I trust this person?
Unfortunately, probably not.
To me, these people are nothing more than a proctor.

I ate a banana today,
It was a good banana.
I'm sure it was healthy,
But really, who is to say.

This could be my Mother.
Do I trust this person?
Of course I do; she is my mother.
I trust her like no other.

I ate a steak today.
It was an amazing steak.
I'm sure it wasn't healthy,
But really, who is to say.

Evidently, the world.
Do I trust the world?
No, not even on a good day.
Not until all information is unfurled.

Who do I trust?
And what is good?
Into this world we are thrust,
And perception is misunderstood.

# The Remembered Dream

I dreamed last night of peace.
A world not divided,
A country that loves one another,
People that understood the future.

This dream was amazing.
This dream was invigorating.

Hope was plentiful,
Everyone was on the same page.
All people worked toward a goal,
And helped everyone achieve.

This dream was captivating.
This dream was stimulating.

In this dream, all things were solved.
Every mystery investigated and entertained.
All things were possible,
And all possibilities existed.

This dream was riveting.
This dream was pivoting.

As with all dreams, I woke.
Into a world of smoke.
But the dream remains.
Even in a world full of hurricanes.

# Can I?

I can feed the world.
I can,
Do you believe me?

It will be easy,
All I have to do is give food to everyone who is hungry.
Pretty simple, right?

We plant food, we raise fish, and we can raise rabbits or some other animal.
This is easy, right?

Evidently, it isn't.
The idea is actually distant.
The world sees hunger as something that cannot be cured.
It sees hunger as something that is assured.

Can we feed from food that is leftover?
Actually, people waste food all over.
We would need to devise an amazing way,
And the masses we would have to sway.

Can this be done?
**No waste in the world**, this would actually be quite fun.
Is it possible?
I don't think it is totally impossible.

Can people invite a family that needs to eat?
This would be an amazing treat.
What if there was one day a week that people shared?
This would be a day to show everyone how much they cared.

I can feed the world.
I can,
Do you believe me?

# The Unexplored

I think of the unexplored.
I consider how much of the world is left.
I think of how much of the world is ignored.
I consider why we are not so deft.

I imagine the vast expanse of the oceans left to explore,
And wonder what we will find.
I doubt anything amazing is in store,
But who knows, I could be one of the not –so- deft and blind.

How many animals are left to discover?
How many plants are undercover?
Are we smart enough to see this vastness?
Are we capable of understanding our daftness?

How do we get there from here?
Is here really a place?
We must analyze our fear,
And journey from this space.

This journey we must take,
To places never before seen.
This will be treacherous, and we must not shake.
By doing this we are able to wean.

This is to say nothing about deep space.
To this vastness, truly, we have not even a taste.
So to the unexplored:
I promise you this: you will not be ignored.

I make it my mission.
To explore every condition.
To find, to search, and be one with the definition,
Having fun, finding every unexplored omission.

# Winning

Winning is great,
But is it important?
I'm not sure.

To win usually makes people happy.
So this is good.
And this is important.

Can you lose and still be happy?
Can the world be a better place with a loss?
I think it can.

It may help someone who needs to win, with a loss.
This is good, Right?

It is good.
So, in effect, winning is not paramount.
It is relative for the situation.

I say this hoping that everyone will see,
In the differences that winning can be.
It is not always important.
It often isn't even prudent.

Would winning a war be an important aspect?
Yes, on this, we must dissect.
If you lose in this, it could be the end.
So winning is definitely something to apprehend.

Winning is great,
But is it important?
Depending on the situation, Yes.

# Dew Drops

Dew drops on a humid morn,
As the day starts before the storm,
All sights seen as the sun rises,
All possibilities open with hopefully very few surprises.

As the mighty storm does approach,
The gusty wind lashes as the mighty clouds broach.
And here I am,
Between the start and the end,
Waiting for the world to transcend.

Dew dropped on a humid morn,
Forgotten in an instant because of a storm reborn.
Does the day remember?
The memory of this should not surrender.

As the mighty storm gales and thrashes,
The lightning thunders and flashes.
And here I am,
In a tempest,
Wishing I were in emptiness.

Dew drops on a humid morn,
Oh, how I wish this day had not been born.
Can I survive this?
Maybe I can, if, of the dew I reminisce.

The world shakes.
The ground now quakes.
And here I am,
Close to flying,
Which is why I am now crying.

Dew drops on a humid morn,
The world being unjustly torn.
As I say, for heaven's sake,
I finally wake.

# Fall as a Day

My favorite day is not a day at all,
It is the beauty that is fall.
For this is a period of change.
To which all things must rearrange.

I always find, I yearn.
For this season to return.
I wonder how many others would say the same.
I wonder how many others this poem will reclaim.

From the turn of the leaves,
To having to put on long sleeves.
This time of year is amazing.
The colors, yellow and orange, are blazing.

This is a time of cooler temperatures, colorful leaves, and seasonal treats.
A time full of phenomenal feats.
As we approach the end of the year,
Gifts, laughter, and joy are both far and near.

The food in the fall is exceptional.
Who we get to eat it with is incredible.
With family and friends, we share memories,
For hours, played like vivid documentaries.

I laugh more at this time of the year than any other.
Visiting with friendships we rediscover.
Oh, what light this day does bring!
And oh, what joy does my heart sing.

Therefore, my favorite day is not a day at all.
It is fall.

# The Minister

About a year ago, I was put on a text chain from a minister.
I am not religious.
I am not religious, in any extent,
But I do believe what is right is right, and what is wrong is wrong.

The messages from the minister are life,
Not terrible, not mean, or filled with strife.
Each held meaning.
Some missed, while others were more intervening.

I found myself day by day thinking of the impact.
Of the joy and happiness that each message would attract.
For the many who see this daily,
And smile gaily.

Some need this text.
Wondering in life what to do next.
Some are lost without a helping hand.
Living today in this strange land.

This life we live is sometimes hard and misunderstood,
But for a second of the day, we are good.
So it is with pleasure when I see this message post.
It is pleasure to think how many are suddenly engrossed.

What hurts me the most about this list,
Is the billions this message has missed.
There are those that do not believe,
But will agree because the first lines they can conceive.

I would like to thank this man.
For doing so much in the world where he can.
Minister Scott, I hope you find each day, and I wish it well.
Thank you, kind sir, for the negativity you repel.

# Changing the World

It brings joy to hear the pitter patter of little feet.
The upbringing of little kids is such a treat.
From the day they are born,
To when they take their first step,
The world has changed.

Mistakes will be made.
Fun games will be played.
Learning will begin.
Some will be doctors,
Others - well, there is no telling.

Worry will abound
From every danger that is around.
Still, it brings joy to my heart
Right from the start.

Kids are funny,
And as gentle as a baby bunny.
They do not know the world.
Parents and teachers must show them
Show them correctly, please.

It is hilarious what kids will say.
It puts me in knots each and every day.
Kids are the future.
So be sure to give the future humor.

Take care of kids,
Be kind to kids,
Teach kids to be kind.
Teach kids to listen.
Teach kids to respect others.

By teaching kids this way,
It shows them that, in life, this is okay.
Change the world.
Teach a child.

# A Thought

Today I fly.
I will fly for hours.
I wonder, how many thoughts I will have.
Could I count them?

What constitutes a thought?
Should I count from when I change a thought?
This is a very thought-provoking question.
One in which I should put in some detection.

I consider my thoughts fascinating,
In a world I find contaminating.
Would others find them as interesting as I do?
Would the world understand them enough to pursue?

Can anyone understand?
Can they be understood?
I sometimes wonder,
I often think the world would be put asunder.

That's it, I need a recorder.
I need a recorder to record every thought.
The recorder could also count.
Give me a screen of statistics with an amount.

Maybe this invention could categorize.
Giving a count of each, which would summarize.
Summarize each thought and then see anew,
Something that, in the whole of the world, no one knew.

Thinking is easy.
Thinking correctly is something not many see.
Don't think small thoughts,
Don't think average thoughts,
Think brilliant thoughts.
Think thoughts to change the world.
Then watch as all thoughts are unfurled.

# Addiction

I am one, which believes, addiction does not exist.
It is a figment of the imagination that is easy to resist.
Some will laugh while others cry.
All should not, for I will tell you why.

This is something fully in the mind.
And because of this, it is easily left behind.
That is impossible, you say.
I do; this is easily done in an easy way.

You say no; it is insanity.
I say no; the mind can easily cease this calamity.
The mind is all-powerful.
Your mind is sophisticated and formidable.

People pay money to treat this "said" addiction.
But I say this is idiotic because it isn't an affliction.
It is nothing more than that the mind,
Could be nothing more than misaligned.

You have the ultimate power over the mind,
It is yours to control and yours to be defined.
You say impossible,
I say this is easy and probable.

You can say to the mind tomorrow, no.
You can tell the mind in which direction it is to go.
All things in life are dictated.
From inside the mind, they are instigated.

For all I have said about the mind,
It takes control and determination to bind.
This is actually an easy start.
Tell the mind this made-up affliction will now part.

I have no addiction.
I do not believe in this affliction.
No matter what the world tells you,
Your mind will always get you through.

So know this:
Addiction is something that does not exist.
It simply can't.
Because the mind can easily resist.

# My Love

My love is boundless,
Sometimes careless,
Often ceaseless,
And can be senseless.

How often have I loved?
What happened to my beloved?
What senseless act is this?
And it all started with a kiss.

Love is funny.
Interesting enough, it laughs at all of us.
This laughter we will discuss
Is often misunderstood and can be treasonous.

My love is caring,
And forever sharing,
Never sparing,
And always daring.

Now back to a kiss,
A memory I am glad I did not miss.
I fell hard that day.
This is when I found my love, and it will never sway.

Heaven looks down from up above,
And a radiant light forms around my love.
For it is indestructible,
And will forever be undeniable.

I Love her,
I adore her.
I worship her.
I need her.

This need is great.
This need is everything, for heaven's sake.
Can life be this good?
Can this love be understood?

# This World That I Know

I know this world is nothing more than a figment of the mind.
For if it were anything more, to the world, I would be blind.
This land is not abstract.
This entire thing is an illusion that will be cracked.

What meaning do these words have?
Can a meaning be defined?
Can the world resolve this meaning?
How many days will humans exist?

Off the wall and to the moon,
I will leave this world soon.
While an illusion, it may be
The setting sun few will see.

Stand up and try to understand.
Relax and realize none of this was planned.
This place is nothing more than a show.
This difficult World that I Know.

I say difficult.

Doom is not doom in a world that knows nothing more.
It is every day,
In everything, in every way.

What hardships have you seen?
What abandonment have you felt?
Were you ever happy?
What is happiness?

I can define each and every one of these.
Actually, very easily.
Would you like me too?
No, in My World, I give this only to a few.

# Being Kind

Being kind is a state of the mind.
It is in all mankind.

It should be taught from the moment a child is born to the time they have finished school.
This is important.
This is something that will help everyone.

Maybe each month we schedule a day of kindness,
To be kind all day long,
Do nice things for people.
Would this put people off from being nice the other days?

Such an easy thing to do,
Often done wrong.
Why?
Because people haven't been taught.

My grandmother and grandfather could have taught them.
Then they would know exactly how to be kind.

Teachers are talented.
Every day, kindness beams from teachers all over the world.
It is amazing,
Showing young little minds how they should be behaving.

I grew up with kindness.
I understood and knew this would bind us.
Kindness, in fact, can be easy.
It is so easy, it is often seen as cheesy.

I find it funny when people do not even know they were kind.
I find it funny when I tell people, and they rewind.
Being kind is often so easy.
Many disregard and are often queasy.

How can people be unkind?
I do not understand this.
It doesn't make sense.

Life is a grand adventure.
Try to be kind to everyone in this venture.
For I do believe in Karma.
For every good deed, it comes back to you tenfold.
This may not be true,
True or not, it seems strange things happen out of the blue.

From within the mind comes the advent of being kind.
This is, in itself, a righteous feeling.
One that is correct and very healing.

I will be able to stand before this god,
And when he says, "Were you kind?"
I will say, **"Yes."**

If I were kind in every way, every day, and every pathway,
What would he say?
"Do you believe?"
At this point, I'd say, "You're kidding me right; I'm standing here talking to you."
After that, I would wonder about his aptitude.

This is where scripture is wrong.
Some of the most unkind people in history have claimed to be Christians.
Being kind in life, good to others, good to animals, and good to the world.
This is good; this is right.

I list many things in life that are important,
Being kind is at the top of this list.
It is one of the most important things in life,
Most important, it can change someone's life.

I believe I have been kind in life,
I try,
I want to be kinder in life,
Can I?

I speak like this because I can.
I speak like this because I am a good man.
Be kind in life,
Please do not cause others strife.

# The Perfect Pizza

I do not know what the perfect pizza is.
I say this because perfect is different depending on taste.

I can say what my perfect pizza would be.
It has a thick crust with butter all over it.
It is spread with homemade tomato sauce and cheese.
With fresh mushrooms, bell peppers, small tomato halves,
spinach, pepperoni, hamburger, and a bit of salt.
Now here is where it gets interesting:
Cook this for a while, then, when it is maybe three minutes from
being done, add fresh onions.
The onions need to be hard on the pizza, not fully cooked.

To me, this is the perfect pizza.
To others, maybe not so much.
Everyone is different.
So when reading anything you disagree with, please do not be
inconsiderate.

# Talent

Many have talent.
Talent comes in many different sizes and shapes.
It can be missed in life.
Life can miss it.

When seen, many will take advantage,
For talent is innate in all of us.
I say this because it is.
Each has a talent that is special.

It may only be special to this one person,
But it is special.

Some talent is perfect.
Some talent needs to be refined.
Others seek affirmation.
From not one or two but a whole nation.

Everyone must find their own talent.
They must seek it out.
For some this will be easy, others very hard.

I have written many, many poems.
I have ideas for a book so grand, it could change the world.
I have inventions that would change everything.
This talent, which I hold in my mind,
Will one day help mankind.

Many have talent.
Many could do the same thing I will do.
Don't miss it.
Don't let life resist it.

# Dinosaurs

I have a question for you.

Are we headed for extinction?
Yes, we are!

You ask why I would say this.
It is estimated that 99.9% of all species that have ever existed are extinct.
This is a crazy number.

Humans are evolving even as I write this.
Take a minute to think about that.
Humans, as Homo sapiens, evolved around three hundred thousand years ago.
This is amazing.

We consider the last two thousand years a long time.
Dinosaurs lived for hundreds of millions of years.
We are nothing more than a small bit of history.
What's even funnier is, some believe, that we were here in the beginning.

The only way for Homo sapiens to continue is to leave this earth.
This is the only way.
Some will disagree.
Please do.

I do not know the path we will eventually take.
It doesn't matter; extinction is something we cannot shake.
I say this not to be sad or mean.
I say this so the path can be seen.

Government's fight,
Corporations fall to greed,
People worry about the wrong things,
Extinction does not care what man brings.

It laughs at us all.
And waits for the last fireball.
We cannot stop any of this.
In fact, this is why I moved to paradise - to live in bliss.

# At the End

I have a bucket list.
In this list were many things.
Almost all have been completed.
In life, I can say I have succeeded.

I have climbed my mountain.
I have swam my sea.
My day has been one of joy.
One that nothing in the world could destroy.

I have seen Stonehenge.
I have explored the town of Bath.
I have visited Windsor Castle,
And built a grand sandcastle.

I have entered Notre Dame.
I have been to the Louvre.
I have stood on the Eiffel Tower,
And stood against an immense wind power.

I have been to the Vatican.
I have stood in the coliseum.
I have been transfixed in the Sistine Chapel.
Mesmerized by what I could not grapple.

I have seen the canals of Venice.
I have drunk the wines of Germany.
I have partied hard in Amsterdam,
And was lucky enough to get out without finding myself in a jam.

I slept in hostels.
I backpacked with almost nothing.
I got my passport stamped in amazing places.
Day by day, covering my bucket list bases.

I have dined in Paris.
Ate Pizza in Rome.
In Amsterdam, I grew so hungry that I ordered plates of food.
And with each one, I was fully skewed.

I have met people from all over the world.
I have been to a toga party in England.
My life has been grand.
This multitude of items is miniscule, you must understand.

Truly, I did most of this in only a month of my life.
How many different lives have I lived?
How many items have I crossed off this list?
I often search for any I may have missed.

All of the above and countless more
Enjoying a life as many have done before.
So with this, I give another,
A bucket list item that took time to discover.

This book, which I hope has brought
Many a deep-questioning thought.
As I close, I do hope you had fun.
For this bucket list item, is done.

There is one more in this book that I did write.
For I started with something that I had to make right.

As I stated,
I leave something with thee,
A promise, an ending to be.

# A Gift

This gift, this book that I have written,
Was nothing more than thoughts I have been given.
Do not worry,
I seek neither wealth nor glory.

These words, in no way, were meant
As evidence.
For I truly plan to live forever.
Hoping for happiness, wherever it may gather.

Many will misinterpret
And consider this a self-portrait.
Every poem has a simple twist.
Nothing more than a moment of here and there, simple bliss.

Words spoken,
Words that are definitely thought-provoking.
Don't worry; do not fear.
I know the end is not near.

Do not hate these words that have been written.
Do not let your heart be frost-bitten.
I write these words as I know some may anger,
But you should not; for the mind, I do not wish to endanger.

Do not let these words take you to some dark place.
They are just words, for heaven's sake.
Darkness was never my intent.
In any extent.

Enjoy, think deep thoughts, and don't worry.
If sorrow you found from this, It was not meant.
At the close, I wish you ado,
And I hope you live a great life, as I do.

Made in the USA
Columbia, SC
30 January 2025

4bda2eba-1dff-4825-82cf-2d143fdbaa74R01